Jonathan Moore

Jonathan Moore is an award winning actor, writer and director. As an actor he has played leading roles at the Royal Shakespeare Co, Royal Court, Donmar, the Royal Exchange and on BBC TV. He has directed theatre and opera world premieres at the Almeida, Donmar, West End, Royal Exchange, Gate, English National Opera, Covent Garden, La Fenice in Venice and on TV among many others. He has directed world premieres by composers such as Turnage, MacMillan, Henze, Schnittke, Nyman, Copeland and more, and his early work was sponsored by Joe Strummer of The Clash. He has collaborated with members of punk band Killing Joke and on several projects with Industrial group Test Dept.

A published playwright and librettist, his work has been performed at leading theatres including the Donmar, Royal Exchange, Gate, BBC TV, radio and internationally. Jonathan was asked by Mark Rylance to direct the large scale immersive project for over fifty performers *What You Will*, a co-production for Shakespeare's Globe, The Cultural Olympiad and Mayor's Office and several subsequent Shakespeare projects. He is due to direct a large scale site specific immersive project for Ludovico Einaudi in Italy and a new opera project with Stewart Copeland. He is on the Artistic Advisory Committee of the Royal Academy of Dramatic Art. He has had a *Who's Who* entry since 2007.

www.jonathanmooreuk.com

First published in the UK in 2015 by Aurora Metro Publications Ltd
67 Grove Avenue, Twickenham, TW1 4HX

www.aurorametro.com   info@aurorametro.com

Inigo © 2015 Jonathan Moore

Cover graphic © 2015 Rhys Jenkins

Introduction © 2015 Mark Lawson

Painting of Ignatius of Loyola by Montserrat Gudiol used by kind permission of Cova, Manresa

Production: Simon Smith

With many thanks to: Neil Gregory, Richard Turk, Grace Thiele, Lucia Tunstall, Ellen Cheshire and Tracey Mulford.

10 9 8 7 6 5 4 3 2 1

Printed by 4Edge Ltd, Hockley, UK

ISBN: 978-1-906582-72-2 (print)
ISBN: 978-1-906582-73-9 (ebook)

INIGO

by

JONATHAN MOORE

With love and thanks to
William "Billy" Hewett SJ
for his initiating inspiration for this play,
and in recognition of his lifetime's devotion
to telling Inigo's story through the arts.

AURORA METRO BOOKS

CONTENTS

Jonathan Moore would like to thank:

Mum and Dad; special thanks to Elly Harrison; Michael Kingsbury and all at The White Bear, especially Jonathan Woodhouse and Rhys Jenkins; all the amazing actors: Ian, Carolyn, Stacie, Christine and all at BADA; Lloyd Trott for invaluable dramaturgical advice and Diane Favell at RADA; Annie Tyson and the young cast at Drama Centre in 2010; Wills at Shakespeare's Globe; Billy Hewett, Jacob Murray, Jack Shepherd, Roger Monk and John Moffat for help with various drafts; Director Greg Hersov and great assistant Rafaella Marcus for editorial help in the rehearsal period. Mark Lawson for all his support; Jane Hellings (and all at Jesuit Media Initiatives.) Andrew Cameron-Mowat SJ, James Martin SJ, Dermot Preston SJ, and Deb Waters for her intelligence and humour and for being a genius prop maker. Chris Smyth and Amber Taylor, our stage managers at the White Bear and Pleasance respectively; Tania Azavedo, assistant director at the White Bear Theatre whose relentless optimism and efficiency lifted everyone. Julie Bergevin, Janice de Broíthe and Chloe France, brilliant assistants for the transfer production. Laura Cordery and Lily Faith Knight, our designers at White Bear and the Pleasance respectively. Ben Cowens, a lighting and sound designer of rare and brilliant gifts.

To the actor Mary D'Arcy Ryan, who was my inspirational drama teacher of genius. (She encouraged my dream when I was ten that I could be an actor). It's all your fault Mary! Love and thanks always. The play reunited us after thirty years and led to her support for the revival; James Garriock, RIP, inspirational headmaster; Tiggy Butler, without whom the first production couldn't have happened; Christina "Potty" Connolly, a major force behind Inigo Enterprises, for her support.

Thanks also to: Cova, Manresa, for granting permission to use the painting of Ignatius of Loyola by Montserrat Gudiol; and to an Anonymous Donor.

Introduction

Saints and Punks: The Theatre of Jonathan Moore

Although I accept that this will not be the case for most travelers in London, the Underground system holds two particular cultural associations for me. When arriving at a station on a particular east-to-west line with green and yellow livery, I think of Seamus Heaney's poetry collection *District and Circle*. And, when catching sight of the warning printed above the door of trains to encourage fluent movement at crowded times – "Obstructing the Doors Causes Delays and Is Dangerous" – I think of the plays of Jonathan Moore.

With a title that captures a crucially combative aspect of both his writing and his personality, *Obstruct the Doors, Cause Delay and Be Dangerous* – one of Moore's early plays – was my introduction to his work in the 1980s, along with a TV version of *Treatment*, his magnificently angry and distinctive piece about Liam, a young man trying to escape from the life of gang violence to which his location and background threaten to condemn him.

Transformation – social, artistic, spiritual – is the recurrent theme of Moore's plays. Apart from Liam's struggle between two possible lives in *Treatment*, the characters in *Fall from Light* have reached the world of opera from a London estate.

Those who know or know about Moore may dare to presume some autobiography in the latter play, as the writer grew up in an ordinary second generation Irish Catholic family and has reached places – such as directing in the grandest opera houses of Europe – that most sociologists would not have predicted to appear on his CV.

Inigo, his tremendous new play, again features a protagonist who ends up somewhere that would originally have seemed unlikely to both himself and to others. Saint Ignatius of Loyola, founder of the Jesuit order of Roman Catholic priests, abandoned a life of wealth, sex and violence to become a Christian pilgrim whose opposition to the greed and theological conservatism of the Vatican made him a frequent target of the Inquisition.

The badge of 'Catholic writer' has become trickier to pin on an author than it was in the middle of the 20th century, when novelists such as Evelyn Waugh, Graham Greene and Muriel Spark declared their religious allegiance in their dust-jacket biographies and in their plots. These days, a more typical example of a Catholic writer might be Hilary Mantel, whose rejection of her childhood faith is reflected in the fact that, in *Wolf Hall* and *Bring up the Bodies*, the Catholic saint, Sir Thomas More, becomes a villain while Thomas Cromwell, one of the architects of the Reformation, is the hero.

Jonathan Moore was born a Catholic and, as someone raised in the same faith, I always recognised him as a Catholic writer in the themes of alteration, redemption, guilt and the curative power of love on which his early plays turned. *Inigo*, though, is clearly his most specifically religious play, although, crucially, the spirit and instincts of the young punk political playwright survive. In common with many Moore characters, Ignatius has aspects of both a saint and a punk.

George Bernard Shaw in *Saint Joan* and Howard Brenton in *Paul* reclaimed two Catholic martyrs for humanism and secularism. But one of the greatest strengths of *Inigo* is that the protagonist is neither the villainous charlatan that Dawkinsesque anti-clerics would prefer him to be nor the sexless simperer that a *Lives of the Saints* for schoolchildren would make him.

And characteristically, for a dramatist whose early plays felt so close to the contemporary that you half expected the actors to have ink on their fingers from the just written scripts, *Inigo*, though historical, is also strikingly a play for today.

Some might consider it luck that Moore happened to be writing about the first Jesuit just as Cardinal Jorge Mario Bergoglio was becoming the first Jesuit pope. But the startling parallels between the scenes in which Ignatius outlines a new church of the poor and pure – and the rhetoric of Pope Francis, who refused to move into the grand pontifical apartments in the Vatican and is seeking to make the Catholic church simpler and humbler – are not a case of Moore being fortunate but of being attuned to historical moods before they happen in the strange way that good writers often are.

Those sequences featuring the Inquisition and the bureaucratic attempts to silence Ignatius also, I think, have deliberate quiet parallels with a contemporary culture in which imposed ideological orthodoxies and witch-hunts have become a feature of many organisations.

The subject of this introduction is Jonathan Moore not me and I include the following detail only because it is so revealing of his nature. I recently experienced a professional crisis (entirely unforeseen and unjust, in the view of both myself and good lawyers) with such physical and psychological consequences that I was for some time not certain of surviving it. On a brief acquaintance that followed from a broadcast appearance together some years ago, John rapidly contacted me to offer support and faith and is high among those to whom I owe my recovery.

His kindness and wisdom during that period revealed the great priest that he might in other circumstances have become, although he might well have struggled with vows of obedience and celibacy – as, which is one of the points of his latest play, did a man now known as St. Ignatius.

Although Jonathan Moore is also a startling director and actor – showing the latter in his terrifying recent Edinburgh

Festival performance in the Paul Sellars verse monologue *Two Graves* – it is a thrill to see him back as a dramatist and with a play as powerfully written, psychologically astute and spiritually nuanced as *Inigo*.

Mark Lawson, May 2015

Mark Lawson writes about culture for *The Guardian* and the *New Statesman* and is theatre critic of *The Tablet*. His work as a broadcaster includes *Front Row* (Radio 4) and *Mark Lawson Talks To...* (BBC4). His novels include *Idlewild* and *The Deaths*.

Author's Note

I'm not a big fan of author's notes. Plays should speak for themselves.

Just a short one then.

Firstly I wrote four drafts of this play when Benedict XVI was Pope. No one had any idea there would ever be a Jesuit Pope. So it all seemed very timely. A Jesuit reformer goes to Rome...

Now an apologia, a *mea culpa*. Or hopefully a Felix Culpa. You can decide.

The play was rigorously historically researched over a long period. However, I have occasionally used dramatic licence with some adjustments of chronology and conflations of characters for the sake of the drama.

As Prospero says at the end of *The Tempest*:

"As you from crimes would pardoned be
Let your indulgence set me free"

Jonathan Moore, London 2015

Biographies

Fayez Bakhsh

The original stage adaption of Jonathan Moore's *Inigo* was Fayez Bakhsh's first role on a fringe theatre stage since graduating from Drama Studio London in 2014. He is both an illustrator and a keen Spoken Word Poet who regularly enjoys demonstrating his ability to combine creative language and a powerful delivery at various events around Reading and London. As Fayez's acting career goes forward he seeks to find challenging work on both stage and screen to approach with all the passion and rigour of an intelligent and determined actor.

Charlie Archer

Charlie trained at RADA, graduating in 2012. His film and television credits include: *Foyle's War*, *We Are Tourists*, and *Lexicon*. His Theatre credits include: *A Mad World My Masters* (RSC/ETT Barbican), *A Midsummer Night's Dream* (Theatre Royal Northampton), The Libertine (Citizens Glasgow/Bristol Old Vic), *A Bright Room Called Day*, *The Illusion* and *Billy Budd* (Southwark Playhouse), and Mark Rylance's *Pop-Up Shakespeare/What You Will* (Shakespeare's Globe, Directed by Jonathan Moore).

Simon Haycock

Simon Haycock trained at Drama Centre, graduating in 2013. His theatre credits include *Coriolanus* and *Troilus & Cressida* with Lazarus Theatre, and *Back* at the Greenwich Theatre. Film credits include *Kaleidoscope Man*, *Love Online* and *Wasp*.

Elle van Knoll

Elle van Knoll started working as an actress at a young age, appearing in TV, film and theatre internationally. Following this, she attained a degree in Criminology and Sociology from Cardiff University. Pursuing her true passion, Elle went on to study at the Academy of Live and Recorded Arts in London and graduated with an MA in Professional Acting in December 2014. Alongside acting, Elle is a playwright who has written for both theatre and screen. She recently set up 'Van Knoll Unlimited', a production company that will be producing Elle's premiere play, *We Just Keep Going* in early September 2015.

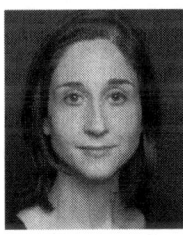

Helena Northcote

A recent graduate of Drama Studio London, Helena Northcote has been working as a voiceover artist and has been in several short films. Most recently she was involved in the RSC Open Stages project at the Ashmolean museum in Oxford.

She is also a writer and is currently developing a one woman show and collaborating on an actor/musician adaptation of medieval stories. Helena is very excited to be making her professional stage debut in this production.

Reggie Oliver

Photo credit Caroline Webster 2015

Reggie Oliver began his career in 1975 at the Grand Theatre, Llandudno in repertory. Since then has worked as actor and director in repertory at Scarborough, Ipswich, Ayr, Cromer and on tour all over the United Kingdom, as well as on BBC Radio and TV. He played in Jonathan Moore's *Street Captives* at Edinburgh and elsewhere in 1980. His West End appearances include *Mr Wilberforce M.P.* (Westminster) *Captain Brassbound's Conversion* (Haymarket) *A Coat of Varnish* (Haymarket & tour) *The Clandestine Marriage* (Albery & tour). Recent theatre work inclues *Stage Frights* (one man show) and sonnet walks for the Globe Theatre (dir. Jonathan Moore).

His published work includes six plays, two novels and six volumes of short stories, which between them have appeared in over fifty anthologies.

Paul Storrier

Paul Storrier trained at the Drama Studio, London, and the Universities of St. Andrews (English) and Oxford (Philosophy/ Theology). His theatre work includes Josef K. (*The Trial*), Wocky (*The Baby*), Steve/ Les (*Decadence*), Horst (*Bent*), Maurice (*Good*), Frank/Geoffrey/Mr. Takei (*Fen*), Prospero (*The Tempest*), Malcom (*Macbeth*), Queen Margaret/Richard (*Richard III*), Creon (*Antigone*). Film work includes title role in *Dave*, and Tony in *Tai Chi Man* (Kelpie Films).

Scott Westwood

Scott trained at the Royal Academy of Dramatic Art.

His theatre credits include: *Tender Napalm* (Albany Theatre), *The Merchant Of Venice* and *Arabian Nights* (Cunard), *A Midsummer Night's Dream* (AMSND14 Open Air), *An Ideal Husband* (Tabard Theatre), *Arcadia*, *A View From The Bridge* and *The Vortex*, (Crescent Theatre Company) and *Hood!* (Peculius Stage).

Scott's training credits include *She Stoops To Conquer*, *Mad To Go*, *The Lady From The Sea* and *Mercury Fur* (RADA).

Ben Cowens (Sound and Lighting Designer)

Ben trained at the Academy of Live & Recorded Arts in stage management & technical theatre specialising in lighting design for theatre, events and dance. Since graduating he has designed and re-lit productions around the United Kingdom and internationally.

Lighting design work includes: *iCoDaCo* (Aberystwyth Arts Centre, Cardiff Dance House and the Suzanne Dellal Centre), *Showtime* (Bridlington Spa), *The Domino Heart* (The Finborough Theatre), *We Happy Few* (The New Diorama Theatre), *Conversations with Dystonia* (The Place), *How to Find Us* (Soho Theatre), *The Story Project 5* (The Arcola) and *Is It Getting Cold in Here...?* (Theatre 503).

Relight work includes: *My People* (Wales Tour), *Speed* (Tristan Bates Theatre), *Snap. Catch. Slam.* (Plough Arts Centre) and *The Snow Spider* (Tristan Bates Theatre).

For more information and up and coming work, please see www.bencowens.co.uk.

Julie Bergevin (Assistant Director)

Julie Bergevin was invited to attend the Claude Watson School for the Performing Arts at the age of 8, in Toronto. She is now an alumnus of the Claude Watson Program, Rosedale Heights School for the Arts, Vanier Company Productions and York University for her honours B.A. in Theatre. In New York she was Stage Management intern for the lab project of *Allegiance*, which will open on Broadway, November 2015. In Toronto, she was Casting intern at JigSaw Casting, head scenic painter at the Lower Ossington Theatre for *Legally Blonde, Joseph, Avenue Q, Spring Awakening, Forever Plaid*, and at Toronto Youth Theatre for *How to Succeed*. She was also set designer for *Spring Awakening* and stage manager for Toronto's production of *A Very Potter Musical*.

Janice de Broíthe (Assistant Director)

Janice holds both a BA in Drama and English and an MA in Drama & Theatre Studies from University College Cork and is a graduate of LAMDA's PG in Theatre Directing. She is the founder and artistic director of Slapdash Theatre and free-lances as a drama facilitator. Directing credits include: *Men Without Shadows* (The Granary, Cork; Players, Dublin); *A Midsummer Night's Dream* (Delta Sensory Gardens, Carlow); *Have A Nice Life* (LAMDA Linbury); *Pint Size* (Edinburgh Festival) and *The Wizard of Oz* (The G.B. Shaw Theatre, Carlow) Assisting credits include: *Earthquakes in London* (Pleasance Islington, Theatr Brycheinhiog, Brecon dir. Sarah Esdaile) and *Single Spies* (Rose Theatre Kingston, dir. Sarah Esdaile).

Chloe France (Assistant Director)

Chloe is a freelance director based in London whose directing credits include *Collective Energy*, Morgan Lloyd Malcom (Hackney Empire); *Red Cross*, Sam Shepard (Albany); *Bazaar and Rummage*, Sue Townsend (C Venues, Edinburgh Fringe). Chloe currently works as an assistant producer with RIFT. Chloe studied History at Magdalene College, Cambridge. Directing credits whilst training include *Cabaret* (ADC Theatre Cambridge), *24 Hour Plays* (ADC Theatre Cambridge) and *Little Shop of Horrors* (Corpus Playroom, Cambridge). *Inigo* is the first show she has worked on at the Pleasance. Chloe's passion is for re-inventing twentieth century texts, or developing new writing, using physical theatre.

Charlie Parham (Assistant Director)

Charlie Parham is a director and writer. He co-founded new theatre company Antic Face, directing its inaugural sell-out production of *Hippolytos* at the V & A Museum.

Other directing credits include: *Coming Back* (Monologue for "Paint Dry"); *Measure for Measure* (America tour); *Ivanov*; *Sophie Scholl* (World Premiere, also writer); *As You Like It* (Edinburgh/London tour); *Waiting for Godot*; *The Priory*; *King Lear* (Europe tour); *Arcadia*; *True West*; *DNA*; *Attempts on her Life*; *The Bald Prima Donna*.

His writing includes *HIV voices*, and he is part of the cabaret drag troupe DENIM, writing and performing with them all over the UK.

Rob Leonard (Fight Director)

Rob's fight directing work includes: *Tamburlaine the Great, Parts 1 & 2* (Fourth Monkey Theatre Company, Jackson's Lane), *Macbeth* (Guildburys, Farnham), *Robin Hood, Spirit of Sherwood* (Chameleon's Web, Colchester), *The Love of the Nightingale* (Courtyard Theatre), *Romeo & Juliet* (Camden Peoples' Theatre), *Roberto Zucco* (Courtyard Theatre), *The Changeling* (Southwark Playhouse), *The Hang of the Gaol* (Brockley Jack), Comedy of Errors (Royal & Derngate Theatre, Northampton, *The Container* (Edinburgh Fringe - Fringe First and Amnesty Awards). Rob is resident stage combat tutor at Italia Conti and on the Fourth Monkey two-year training programme, and teaches regularly at Royal Central School of Speech & Drama. He has worked in several other drama schools, and taught workshops across the UK, in Germany and the US.

Siân Williams (Choreographer)

Siân Williams trained at the London College of Dance and Drama. She founded The Kosh dance theatre company with Michael Merwitzer.

Siân has worked as choreographer for Shakespeare's Globe Theatre since 1999, as Movement Director for the Royal Shakespeare Company, and is a member of The Factory Theatre Company.

Credits

Inigo had its World Premiere at the White Bear Theatre, London on February 3rd 2015, and transfers to the Pleasance Theatre from May 25th 2015.

Fayez Bakhsh – Inigo
Elle van Knoll – Catalina/Magdalena/Woman/Arteaga
Paul Storrier – Carafa/Jean Chanon/Pedro de Loyola
Charlie Archer – Martin de Loyola/Xavier/Salim/Calisto
Simon Haycock – Blacksmith/Kinsman 2/Bobadilla/
Roderigo (Gentleman with club)/Conversini.
Helena Northcote – Isabel Roser/Maria
Reggie Oliver – Figueroa/Del Hoyo/Ardevol
Scott Westwood – Favre/Carlo/Hernandez (Depressed man)/Kinsman 1/Corregidor

Director: Jonathan Moore
Sound and Lighting Designer: Ben Cowens
Set and Costume Designer: Lily Faith Knight
Choreographer: Siân Williams
Fight Director: Rob Leonard
Assistant Directors: Julie Bergevin, Janice Louise de Bróithe, Chloe France and Charlie Parham.
Stage Manager: Amber Taylor
Prop Maker: Deb Waters

Additional White Bear credits:

Timothy Block – Figueroa/Del Hoyo/Ardevol
Tom Durant-Pritchard – Martin de Loyola/Xavier/
Salim/Calisto
Matthew Howell – Favre/Carlo/Hernandez (Depressed man)/Kinsman 1/Corregidor
Hilary Tones – Isabel Roser/Maria

Set and Costume Designer: Laura Cordery
Fight Director: Bret Yount
Assistant Directors: Rafaella Marcus and Tania Azevedo
Stage Manager: Chris Smyth

INIGO

Jonathan Moore

Alphabetical List of Characters

With the exception of Inigo, all other parts can be shared amongst an ensemble of eight upwards.

ARTEAGA

BEAUTIFUL WOMAN (at Castle Loyola)

BLACKSMITH (Martin)

CALISTO

CARLO CARAFA

CARNIVAL GOERS

CLERK (Salamanca trial)

CONVERSINI

CORREGIDOR (Homctown judge)

DEL HOYO

FIGUEROA

FRANCISCO XAVIER

LAINEZ, RODRIGUES and SALMERON (First Jesuits)

GIAN CARAFA

GUARD (Alcala)

HERNANDEZ (Depressed man)

INIGO

ISABEL ROSER

JEAN CHANON

2 KINSMEN (del Hoyo's)
LITTLE BOY INIGO (May be treated as imaginary)
MAGDALENA (Inigo's sister-in-law)
MARIA (Inigo's wet-nurse)
MARTIN DE LOYOLA
MASTER ARDEVOL
MESSENGER (to Carafa)
NICOLAS BOBADILLA
NOTARY (Figueroa's)
NOTARY (Conversini's)
PAGE (to Conversini)
PEDRO DE LOYOLA
PETER FAVRE
PRINCESS CATALINA
RODERIGO (Gentleman with club)
SALIM (Moor)

NB Some sections of optional dialogue are marked with brackets and grey text.

ACT ONE

LOYOLA. BASQUE REGION.
1496. DARKNESS.

We hear the sound of loud hammering. Metal on metal. Out of the dark comes a light glowing like a galaxy in space. We see gradually it is a blacksmith's forge.

The BLACKSMITH (MARTIN DE ERRAZATI) stripped to the waist, wields a hammer high above his head. A LITTLE BOY of about five, INIGO, watches him.

BLACKSMITH *(smashing the hammer)* So. That's. How. We. Do it. Little Inigo. We need to get it good and hot. Then smash it into shape while we can. Smash it while its white hot. Then we can make of it what we want. But we must keep refining, get the impurities out. Now watch this!

MARIA enters.

MARIA   Martin. We told you not to let him come into the forge. It's dangerous. He doesn't belong here. And our children play too rough. He's noble. Sensitive. Come on Inigo. Back in the house. *(She takes INIGO into her arms)*

BLACKSMITH You'll spoil him, Maria. He's tougher than you think. You're just his wet-nurse, love. Anyone would think you were his real mum.

MARIA   Well I'm all the mother he's ever had. Aren't I, Inigo? Eh? *(Sings to him a Basque lullaby)* "Loyolako, Txikie, Loyolako Txikie." *(Little Loyola, little Loyola)* Mummy's gone to Heaven but Maria loves you, eh?

BLACKSMITH goes back to hammering.

Lights cross fade to:

STREET CORNER OUTSIDE A TAVERN. AZPEITIA. BASQUE REGION. 1515.

A carnival. Mardi Gras. Loud music. Masked revellers celebrate.

A MAN IN A MASK comes rushing in. He removes his mask. It is INIGO.

His brothers, PEDRO and MARTIN DE LOYOLA are waiting for him with tankards, drunk. During the scene he dusts himself down and fastidiously checks his highly fashionable appearance. He uses a pocket mirror to see:—

His beautiful long hair. Doublet and hose. Long sword and short dagger. Fine shoes. All is in expensive materials. He looks every inch the courtier. A contrast with his less resplendent looking brothers, though they are gentlemen. They drink throughout the scene, refilling their tankards from a large flagon.

MARTIN   Hey little brother!

PEDRO   Where's the fire, Inigo? What's happened?

INIGO   Had to make a quick retreat from an angry father. The Del Hoyo girl –

PEDRO and MARTIN make salacious noises.

MARTIN   Did you –

PEDRO   You lucky little pig. I've been after her for years.

MARTIN   That's what I love about you Pedro. You may be a priest but you're still well – a hombre.

PEDRO AND MARTIN *(toast)* To Hombres!

MARTIN *(sees INIGO's wound)* Hey! You've been hurt. Was that Del Hoyo? Let's get him!

INIGO   Martin – She's his daughter. He's right to be offended. *(Of wound)* It's nothing anyway.

MARTIN   Little brother. The runt of the litter and already so brave, eh?

PEDRO *(hands him a tankard)* Get that down you.

INIGO   Thanks. *(He drinks deep)*

PEDRO   So what was she like?

INIGO   Who?

MARTIN   The Del Hoyo floozy.

INIGO   Just doesn't feel right talking about her like that. Not honourable.

PEDRO   Quite the little courtly gentleman.

MARTIN   Where he got his airs and graces. Certainly didn't get them at the blacksmith's foundry. Well, you might think you're too good for running the family estate but since Daddy died—

INIGO   That's your job now.

PEDRO   "The man of the house."

INIGO and PEDRO snigger.

MARTIN   Yes. That's right.

INIGO   I love coming back home to visit. I do love it here. The Basque people. The air. The earth. But after the sheer... scale of Arevalo and Navarette and the castles. Real Palaces. Like in the story books. Places where the noble Knight Amadis de Gaul might have lived.

MARTIN   Oh God here we go again with Amadis de bloody Gaul.

PEDRO   He's obsessed!

INIGO   That's enough you two. Yes. A real palace with real knights. Banquets. Jousting. The finest of duelling instructors. I am now a most excellent swordsman. One of the best.

MARTIN   Not too grand for a kick up the backside, boy.

INIGO   Its all just so much... more. And the ladies—

PEDRO AND MARTIN Mmmm.

INIGO   No, not what you're used to. But real Ladies. And one particular Lady – one very special Lady... *(catches himself)*

PEDRO   Yes? Did you have her?

INIGO *(sudden flash of intense anger)* Shut your mouth, Pedro! *(He draws his sword)* I will not have you dishonour her, sir.

PEDRO   Alright, alright I'm only playing with you. God, your temper boy.

MARTIN *(slaps INIGO's head)* If I ever see you draw your sword on a Loyola again, especially the pious Padre here, you'll have me to answer to.

INIGO   You even sound like Daddy now.

MARTIN *(smiles)* Good impression, isn't it? I've been working on it.

This breaks the tension. They all laugh.

MARTIN, PEDRO AND INIGO *(like their Father)* "You'll have me to answer to!"

MARTIN   The Loyolas!

They raise their tankards.

MARTIN, PEDRO AND INIGO The Loyolas! The best!

MARTIN   So. Mardi Gras, boys.

INIGO   Yes!

PEDRO   O Yes! In recognition of our weaknesses, Holy Mother Church has allowed us a night of Carnival.

MARTIN   Pedro, If it isn't about Knights, jousting, duelling and wooing a Lady – Inigo isn't interested.

INIGO   We're all church goers. Believers. But we shouldn't let it spoil our fun.

MARTIN   So who's in for a night of serious wenching and gambling then?

INIGO   You forgot dancing. And fighting.

MARTIN   Alright, who's in for a night of serious fun – wenches, gambling and dancing. And fighting.

MARTIN, PEDRO AND INIGO *(chanting)* Loyola! Loyola! Loyola!

A VOICE   Sons of whores! *(They stop)*

MARTIN *(to INIGO)* You said that without moving your lips.

A VOICE   I say, you are a son of a whore.

INIGO and PEDRO become aware that DEL HOYO and two KINSMEN are behind MARTIN, who cannot see them yet.

MARTIN   You just did it again. *(Beat)* They're behind me, aren't they?

INIGO and PEDRO nod together.

MARTIN *(turns to face the new arrivals and calls across to them)* Well. Well. Well. What have we here? The poxy old Galician himself. Del Hoyo.

PEDRO   What do you want Señor Del Hoyo?

DEL HOYO   Satisfaction.

MARTIN   Well there's an excellent bordello a bit down the street, sir.

DEL HOYO   I'll leave that to you and your degenerate priest, Loyola.

MARTIN   You insult my brother, sir?

DEL HOYO   Indeed I do. I insult you, your priest and most of all your youngest Loyola for dishonouring my daughter. Mask or no mask. Inigo, I believe the runt is called.

INIGO   Martin. Signor Del Hoyo. I fear I may indeed have offended you.

MARTIN   "Inigo the Diplomat".

INIGO   How may I assuage your just anger, sir?

DEL HOYO   Nothing but your death.

INIGO strides alone to face them.

INIGO   We're Basques, sir. And we do more than we talk. I have tried to seek for peace. But you will have none other than my blood. But once more I offer it. What may I do without dishonour to assuage your sense of offence in this?

DEL HOYO   Blood is all I want.

They unsheathe their swords and the MARDI GRAS STREETFIGHT ensues. This should be quite a savage and stylised fight with swordplay but also a more 'street-fighting' style. Head butts, gouging, kneeing. It shouldn't feel like a glamorous, swashbuckling scene (although the swordplay is impressive, especially INIGO's), instead it should be raw, dangerous and messy. Carnival-goers get caught up in the action.

INIGO dons a mask – followed by the other brothers as CARNIVAL-GOERS get caught up in the fight which develops into a full-stage mêlée.

THE WATCH arrives and breaks it up.

Lights fade.

We hear the sound of MARIA singing the lullaby "Little Loyola" the BLACKSMITH, MARTIN is seen hammering at the forge, the last hammer blow coincides with CORREGIDOR'S (judge's) hammer as we cross fade into:

COURT 1515. INIGO IN DOCK.

PEDRO and MARTIN look on.

CORREGIDOR Inigo Lopez de Loyola, you have heard the charges against you for enormous and premeditated crimes. Your behaviour warrants the severest penalty at my disposal. However as the Loyolas are patrons of the churches at Azpeitia and Azcoitia they seem to have taken an insurance for you and claim you are, or have been, a 'tonsured cleric'. Well we all know that's expediency. To get you off the hook, eh?

You seem to have influential friends, young Loyola.

We must bow to this pressure it seems. But I would like to state that this is a sad abuse of canonical powers, this is a sorry miscarriage of justice and your richly deserved punishment has been avoided. Prisoner discharged.

INIGO   Thank you sir.

CORREGIDOR Now go. For now. *(He leaves)*

PEDRO and MARTIN cheer, then greet INIGO.

MARTIN   Told you we'd do what was needed, Inigo.

INIGO   Thanks Martin, thanks Pedro.

Lights fade.

Off in the distance we see LITTLE BOY INIGO and BLACKSMITH at his furnace in the dark and hear the lullaby. The smashing of the last hammer blow coincides with a huge explosion. Scene changes to:

SIX YEARS LATER. PAMPLONA CITADEL. BATTLEMENT. MAY 24TH 1521.

INIGO stands high on the walls of the citadel. Sound of whizzing cannonballs and battle. He is shouting to a handful of men.

INIGO   We have the glory in our hands today. We were told it was impossible to hold this citadel for more than one hour. Madness. Three days later – we are still here! A handful of men against a whole battalion of the enemy. And you are good men. Men loyal to your Lord and countrymen. But don't give up. Don't falter even for a second. Don't let the enemy find one small crack in our citadel. Because that's what he wants. One tiny crack and he will break in and destroy us. Let us raise our Standards and show the enemy we are men of glory and honour. Let us bravely and generously answer the call of the King. Show his Majesty that he has soldiers who can do the impossible. We have the honour! We have the glory!

Cheers. Sound of a cannon firing. INIGO falls to the ground.

All sound cuts out. Silence.

In the darkness we hear the Basque lullaby.

Lullaby: Loyolako Txikie, Loyolako Txikie.

SICKBED. LOYOLA HOME. 1521.

INIGO is in bed. A wintry landscape outside the window.

INIGO   Magdalena! Magdalena! *(He rings a bell)*

MAGDALENA, his sister-in-law, comes in.

INIGO   You took your bloody time. I am stuck in this bed, you know. Do you think I'd stay in this hole otherwise?

MAGDALENA   What is it now, Inigo?

INIGO   No need to be snappy Magdalena. Isn't there anything decent to read? In the whole house?

MAGDALENA   You have plenty that's decent to read.

INIGO   Decent? Yes that's the problem. *The Lives of the Saints? The Life of Christ?* I mean – no offence Magdalena, but –

MAGDALENA   I brought those books with me from the Court. They are beautiful, Inigo. Profound.

INIGO   I know, Magdalena and I appreciate it but I've been months in this bed now and I'm so bored. And utterly useless. Pathetic. Weak.

MAGDALENA   You're lucky to be alive.

INIGO   Well perhaps luckier if I wasn't.

MAGDALENA   I thought you had a bit more to you than that.

INIGO *(suddenly snaps angrily)* Oh did you? Well I'm sorry to disappoint you. Sorry I survived. *(Pause)* I apologise Magdalena. But hearing you mention Court just makes me realise how much I miss it. All I'm asking for are some books about chivalry. Honour. Courtly love. Amadis De Gaul. Duelling. Romance. Not all these dusty old saints. I admire them but they're all so impossibly good. It was alright for them but this is the modern world.

They never did a thing wrong their whole lives. They came straight out of the womb and floated onto a stained glass window. No lusts for them. No weakness. And no bloody fun. No dancing. No gambling. No duelling. Everything that makes life... life. I don't like saints. I admire them. Pray to them even. Can't say I'd like to have a drink with any of them.

MAGDALENA That's all there is, Inigo. We have no other books in the castle.

MARTIN enters with PEDRO.

PEDRO   How's the invalid?

MARTIN   Poor little runt.

INIGO   Oh I'm having a wonderful time. Never better. Any more stupid questions?

MARTIN   You'll soon be up on your feet in doublet and hose dancing and chasing girls again. *(Kisses MAGDALENA on the cheek.)* Of course, my sweet, those days are over for me now. Inigo's still single. He can do what he likes. Lucky toad!

MAGDALENA Thanks Martin.

MARTIN   Not a day do I regret the union of our two illustrious families, my darling.

INIGO   Her illustrious family you mean.

MARTIN   Loyola is still a proud name, sonny. And stop being so bad tempered.

INIGO   I'm not bad tempered.

MARTIN   Yes you are.

INIGO   I said I'm not bad tempered. Understood?

MARTIN   It's your own fault.

INIGO   Why? It's not my fault the French doctor set my leg all wrong. I didn't want it broken and reset again.

PEDRO   Not the first time, no. But you didn't have to risk your life and get them to break and reset it yet another time. Just so your leg would look good in doublet and hose again. The vanity of it.

MARTIN   What was wrong with a bit of sticky out bone?

MAGDALENA   I think you were very brave Inigo. I'll never forget it. Not once did you cry out even as they sawed through that protruding bone.

INIGO   It was the honourable and knightly thing to do.

MARTIN   It was the mad thing to do.

MAGDALENA   Come along, Martin. We don't want to tire the patient out.

MARTIN *(as they leave)* And get better soon. For all our sakes.

INIGO   Thanks Martin. Thanks Pedro. For nothing.

He picks up one of the books. Flicks through it. Casts it aside. He sits there, bored. He closes his eyes.

Lights change subtly. A sense of music. A beautiful WOMAN appears in his imagination in the room. INIGO sits up in bed.

INIGO   Who are you?

WOMAN   You know who I am. You saw me at the joust at the Duke of Najera's castle.

INIGO *(enjoying the fantasy, the formal language and ritual of Courtly love)* The Princess Catalina! Forgive me, most noble, royal and wond'rous Lady but due to my incapacitation I am not able to perform the most fitting and decorous demonstration of my respect and admiration for you.

CATALINA   Forgiven, worthy Knight. I am imprisoned and forlorn. Will you save me, Inigo Lopes de Loyola?

INIGO   If it be my death, my Lady. Though it be madness, danger and oblivion I face. I will endure the most extreme trials for you. I dare all for you.

CATALINA   Inigo, Inigo, Inigo. *(She disappears)*

INIGO   My Lady! My Lady! Please come back. *(He looks around the room)* Oh God if I could just get out of bed and walk around for a while. Magdalena! Magdalena! *(Rings bell, gets no response)*

Mmm. Don't blame them for not coming. They're probably sick and tired of me. *(Looks round)* Mmm. *Lives of the Saints. (He idly flicks through 'The Lives of The Saints')* What's this in the introduction? "The Saints were the Knights of God"? Knights, eh? *(Flicks through book)* Living on nothing but herbs and water. Mmm. Delicious. Why would they do that? What would that look like? What would it feel like? Can I even begin to imagine that? *The Life of Christ. (Inigo picks up book, reads)*

"Imagine you are there. As if the events in this book are happening now". O well. Nothing better to do. Let's see... *(He closes his eyes)*

Lights fade. Time lapse.

BLACKSMITH swings hammer in the forge. The wet-nurse MARIA sings lullaby:– Loyolako Txikie.

We see the LITTLE BOY INIGO

Lights up on:

INIGO IN BED

INIGO *(flicks through book)* Saint Francis. O yes. He was a first rank kind of saint I suppose. The best. He'd be the one to beat. People loved him. Children loved him. Animals loved him. He gave everything away. All his riches. He even gave away his fine clothes and swapped with a poor beggar. Mmm. Why would someone do that? Could I ever do something like that? What if I did? I've always been up to a challenge. But new ones, eh? Fasting? Penance? Extreme trials and quests. Rigorous. Heroic. What if... What if... *(He closes his eyes)*

Lights fade. Time lapse.

The BLACKSMITH smashes hammer in the forge. We hear the lullaby again.

Lights back to:

INIGO IN BED

INIGO   My Lady. My Lady.

The PRINCESS CATALINA appears to him again in his imagination.

CATALINA   Yes?

INIGO *(fights for the words)* I... I... I have no words for you.

CATALINA   No?

INIGO   No. Not today. I'm sorry.

CATALINA   You abandon me?

INIGO   No. No. It's just...

CATALINA   Farewell Inigo Lopes de Loyola.

INIGO   My Lady!

CATALINA disappears.

INIGO   What's happening to me? When I fantasise about the Royal Lady and worldly triumphs I enjoy it at the time but afterwards I'm left – so... empty. When I do the same about the saints and outdoing their exploits I've noticed that the joy lasts. What's happening to me? I don't want this. This change. Who knows where it will lead? This pain. I feel as if I'm being broken again. My soul. Broken and reset like my leg. Hammered into a new shape. By God? Or the Enemy? Circling my citadel to find a breach in my walls. Which is which? What's happening to me?

Lights cross fade. Time lapse.

The BLACKSMITH smashes his hammer in the forge. We hear the lullaby.

Lights cross fade to:

INIGO asleep in bed. He wakes up. He has sensed something. He sees something. It is clear he is having a vision.

Lights cross fade. Time lapse.

INIGO in a chair. Looking out of a window. Projection of a vast starscape.

INIGO *(calm)* Look up. Look up at the stars. Consider the stars. They have no plans. No vainglory. But they are the brightest explosions of love. Forged in the smithy of God's mind. Here, outside my window, over the hills of Onazmendi they shine more beautifully than any Emperor's robes. Suspended in perfect trust of God's good space. Thank you for the stars. Thank you for showing them to me as if for the first time. Same old sky. But new eyes.

Lights fade. Music.

We see and hear the BLACKSMITH smash his hammer.

Time lapse.

Basque folk music plays. Out of the darkness a light comes up on the window in INIGO's room. It is spring outside.

The light widens to reveal:

INIGO'S ROOM

INIGO walks across the room with a stick. He is carrying a homemade book. He sits at his desk. Opens the book and copies from one book into another. MAGDALENA enters.

MAGDALENA   Inigo.

INIGO   Ah Magdalena.

MAGDALENA   How's the book progressing?

INIGO   Look. I've copied all Jesus' words in red ink and Our Lady's in blue. Look at the lettering! You won't find much better calligraphy than that. This must be the best book of its kind. Anywhere.

MAGDALENA   The best? What matters is that it is beautiful Inigo. I'm so glad you've finally got something to keep you occupied. You hardly ever ring that bell now.

INIGO   These books. It's all − shining new. Yes I've read the stories before. Always liked them but I've never seen the words like this before. I can really see the stories in my imagination. I can really feel them.

MAGDALENA   This is a grace, Inigo.

INIGO   Just feel different, Magdalena. Everything's changed. Forever. I don't belong here any more. I... have made secret plans.

MAGDALENA   Then go. Go Inigo.

INIGO   You though. What will you do?

MAGDALENA   I will stay. I swore in front of God to marry Martin and I must stay here. It's my duty. But you Inigo. You should follow your heart.

INIGO *(pause)* Well I've been thinking − I would like to visit...

MAGDALENA   Where?

INIGO *(smiles, shy)* Our Lady's shrine at Aranzazu. A pilgrimage. *(They look at each other. Start laughing)* I know. I can't believe it either.

MAGDALENA I'm glad my books were of some small use after all! Look at you now. When I first met you – I thought you were a big headed typical arrogant Macho Hombre.

INIGO You were right! I was. And much worse. But my other plans must remain secret. Don't tell Martin. You know. About the – well, the change in me.

MAGDALENA He knows.

INIGO You haven't told him?

MAGDALENA Of course not. But the whole house knows. Everyone can see.

INIGO Yes. *(With difficulty)* I just – I just – want to see if I can be like one of those – well – one of the knights from the Lives of The Saints. The *Flos Sanctorum*. A 'Knight for God' as the introduction has it. Do both. Be Amadis the Knight but in a new way. Does that sound mad, Magdalena?

MAGDALENA Yes. *(They laugh, and MAGDALENA looks at him tenderly)* No Inigo. It sounds beautiful.

INIGO I've loved having someone to discuss all this with.

MAGDALENA Me too, Inigo. Someone to open my heart to about my dreams. My sadness.

INIGO Oh Magdalena – how can I help?

MAGDALENA You must escape. Be something else. Something more. Follow your dream, Inigo. Do it for both of us.

INIGO But then what?

MAGDALENA Some great adventure of the soul is happening to you. But take a breath, Inigo! You must know the story of the Grail Knights? Who had to enter the forest in a new way on a new path to a destination as yet undisclosed? This was their only path to enlightenment.

INIGO Yes. Yes.

MAGDALENA   God knows the way, Inigo. Because He is the way. Trust in Him.

Lights fade. Music.

Lights up on:

A ROOM IN LOYOLA CASTLE, 1522.

MARTIN   Can't you talk to him Pedro?

PEDRO   It's just a phase. He'll come round again.

MARTIN   Yes, but he told one of the servants to find out about the Carthusian Monastery in Seville. Where they live on nothing but herbs. And he said it wasn't extreme enough.

PEDRO   He was just making enquiries.

MARTIN   I love the little runt. I don't want to lose him, Pedro.

PEDRO   Give him some time.

MARTIN   Why can't he just be a bit more like you? I mean you may be a priest but you're still –

PEDRO   'An hombre?'

MARTIN   What's the matter with you now?

PEDRO   Nothing. I just envy his – zeal. His first rush of love. I remember that.

INIGO enters. He is dressed again in courtly attire. Breastplate. Red cap. Multicoloured cape. Sword and dagger. Beautiful golden-red hair. He walks with a limp, which he would have for the rest of his life.

INIGO   Well. My horse is prepared. Please give it to one of the servants. I'm going by mule. I wanted to say farewell.

MARTIN   Now he's going by mule. A Loyola on a mule! Never. You can't be serious about this.

PEDRO   Inigo. Go on your pilgrimage. Then see. Go gently. Don't rush into anything. Try not to take everything so seriously.

INIGO *(gentle)* Like you Pedro?

PEDRO   Yes. Perhaps.

INIGO   With your battles with the nuns of the convent, your intrigues, your mistress. That manner of gently?

PEDRO   Inigo –

INIGO   Well, it isn't about doing what's easy, Pedro. It's about following a tough road. It's about heroic choices. It's about doing everything for God. Hard, strong love and self-denial. That's what it's about, Pedro.

PEDRO   Don't lecture me Inigo. Not from your position of rash enthusiasm based on a three month conversion.

INIGO   Nine months.

PEDRO   Three months. Nine months. Try ten years. Try fifteen. Let's see how easy you find dealing with your new-found zeal in the real world. When the fire's cooled. When your weaknesses rear up to bite you on the backside. When you get tired of being in your own skin. Tired of trying to be decent and the dull ache of failure always rumbling somewhere in your guts as you try to live up to an impossible standard. Cold. Ugly. And painfully thrown in your face as its just not humanly possible to be perfect, little brother.

INIGO   Not humanly possible, no.

PEDRO   Oh please. You sanctimonious little prig.

MARTIN   See? See what you've done Inigo? Is this what your god of peace and love wants?

INIGO   "I have come with a sword. To set brother at variance with brother."

PEDRO   Ah, the seasoned novice.

MARTIN   Look we all believe in God, Inigo. Us Loyolas have always been respectable church goers. But there are limits. God's a reasonable, decent sort of chap. He's not about shaking everything up and causing trouble.

INIGO   Really?

MARTIN   Think what you're throwing away. Your share of the Estate. Its disrespect for your family.

INIGO   "Who is my family? Who are my mother, brothers? Anyone who hears my will and does it is my father, mother and brothers."

MARTIN   Go on. Get out then.

INIGO   Goodbye.

MARTIN goes over to INIGO. Slaps him in the face. INIGO bridles. After an inner struggle, he turns the other cheek and presents it to MARTIN to strike.

MARTIN   Oh no. You really have taken all this to heart haven't you? *(INIGO is silent)* Yes. Well how about this? *(He punches INIGO. INIGO bristles. Eyes flashing with anger)*

PEDRO   Martin. Stop it now.

MARTIN   He wants to draw his sword. I can smell it. I can see it in his eyes. He's still a Loyola after all. Go on then. *(MARTIN punches him again. INIGO struggles with all his might not to respond)* Go on. And again. *(Punches INIGO. Again no response)* Runt. Idiot. Fool. *(With each word he punches, kicks and slaps INIGO. Still no response)*

PEDRO   Enough Martin. Enough.

MARTIN shoves PEDRO away.

MARTIN   Plague-pit priest.

PEDRO   Martin.

MARTIN *(continues to hit INIGO)* Come on! Come on! Fight back. Fight back you bastard. Be a man. Show some honour!

INIGO begins to vomit as he represses his deeply ingrained impulse to violence.

PEDRO   Stop this at once, Martin.

MARTIN   Well. If you insist. I'm sorry Inigo. I just wanted to see how serious you are. I have a little farewell gift for you, Inigo. Just to show there are no hard feelings.

INIGO *(stares in surprise at MARTIN)* Martin. Do you really –

MARTIN   Of course. I respect your decision. *(Beat)* Come in now, my dear.

A beautiful WOMAN enters. She moves over to INIGO.

WOMAN   Inigo?

MARTIN   Show him what he'll be missing.

PEDRO   Martin, is this really necessary?

INIGO   Please, Martin. *(The WOMAN strokes INIGO's hair)* Please, madam. *(She strokes his face. INIGO fights himself. She moves herself seductively in front of him. Kisses his face. INIGO resists. Finally he strokes her hair)*

INIGO   So beautiful.

MARTIN   That's more like it! Welcome back Inigo.

INIGO   You are very beautiful. I want to love... you. The soul of you. *(He says this with such gentle simplicity, and lack of any possible earlier trace of moral superiority, that she is taken aback)* Don't let them use you like this. You are in pain. You have suffered from men and their cruelty. Men like me. And I'm so sorry. *(He smiles and kisses her on the forehead. She looks startled. Looks over to MARTIN–)*

MARTIN   Out bitch!

INIGO   Don't talk to her like that.

MARTIN   Go on, get out!

The WOMAN runs away.

INIGO *(quiet)* I love you too, you know, Martin.

MARTIN   You've always been too good for us, haven't you? Go on then. Get out. I will not have you making the honourable name of Loyola a thing of disgrace in the world. From now on you are dead. *(He spits in INIGO's face and marches off)*

PEDRO   Martin!

PEDRO goes over to INIGO. Tenderly wipes his face.

INIGO *(warmly)* Thanks Pedro. I will pray for you. *(He leaves)*

PEDRO is left on his own, profoundly disturbed and shaken.

PEDRO   Do. Please do, little Loyolako Txikie.

Lights fade.

The sound of the beautifully plaintive Islamic call to prayer floats across the air.

A ROAD. FEBRUARY 1522. INIGO ON A MULE.

A MOOR joins him.

MOOR   *Salaam*, my friend. May I join you?

INIGO   You may. Fine horse, sir.

MOOR   I am Salim.

INIGO   My name is... The Pilgrim.

SALIM   Ah. On pilgrimage?

INIGO   Yes. To Our Lady's shrine. Montserrat.

SALIM   Ah yes. Miriam. A most Holy Lady.

INIGO   I'm glad to hear you say that, brother.

SALIM   Of course. She is an important figure to us Muslims. As is Isa – your Jesus.

INIGO   We are all the children of God, brother.

SALIM   We are indeed. *(Pause)* I was wondering...

INIGO   Yes?

SALIM   Your faith decrees that the Holy Miriam was a virgin when she conceived Jesus?

INIGO   Yes.

SALIM   Please explain.

INIGO   It can't really be explained, Salim. It is a miracle. It's inexplicable.

SALIM   Is it very important that she was a virgin, Pilgrim?

INIGO   To us it is, Salim.

SALIM   Why, Pilgrim?

INIGO   Because – because – she was without sin.

SALIM   It is a sin to conceive a child?

INIGO   No – well – yes. It's original sin, isn't it?

SALIM   What is original sin, Pilgrim?

INIGO   I'm not absolutely sure to be honest. I'm no theologian. But... We are – we – well. We're born sinful then we can wash that away with God's help. I think.

SALIM   I can accept the miracle of the virgin conception.

INIGO   Good.

SALIM   It is powerful. Inexplicable, as you say, but powerful.

INIGO   Indeed.

SALIM   For God, nothing is impossible.

INIGO   Good man, Salim.

SALIM   But – anatomically –

INIGO Yes?

SALIM It all depends on how one defines virginity of course but how – at least at the level of one physical definition – could she be a virgin after she's given birth?

INIGO It's God's wonderful poetry. The miracle of life.

SALIM Isn't all life miraculous?

INIGO Yes. Yes. It is. It's not just about basic physical definitions, man.

SALIM I still can't see it, Pilgrim. Please explain.

INIGO It's about faith in the end.

SALIM It's getting late. The road forks to my village, Pedrola, just a bit further ahead. It was good talking to you. God be with you, Pilgrim. *(He moves off)*

INIGO Interesting. I wish I'd made a better argument about it. Wish I had the learning. Did I let you down, Our Lady? Should I have defended your honour? He did insult you after all, my Lady. He did. *(He draws his sword)* I will find him and I will kill him for so dishonouring you.

(INIGO confused, anxious) But is it right? To kill. Ever? Is it what God wants me to do? No. What's happening to me? Everything used to be so clear. Honour offended: Duel. Satisfaction. Easy. Now everything's so strange and complicated.

What's this? The road forks. Left is Pedrola where the Moor said he was going. The other the High Road to Montserrat. What shall I do? God – show me. Show me. No? Right. That's it. Over to you Lord. I'm going to let the reins go.

(He does so) If you want me to spare the Moor take me on the High Road. If I should stab him – let the mule follow the Moor to the village. Ah. Here we go. Off up onto the

High Road. O well. *(He sheathes his sword)* The Moor and his descendants shall live.

The sound of monks chanting.

Lights up on:

THE CELL OF JEAN CHANON, A FRENCH BENEDICTINE MONK AT MONTSERRAT. MARCH, 1522

JEAN is kneeling in prayer. INIGO enters, still resplendent in his knightly clothes.

INIGO   Bless me, Father. I have sinned.

JEAN   What do you seek in Montserrat?

INIGO   I'm a sinner and I need to go to confession.

JEAN   Yes. I am Jean. Jean Chanon.

INIGO   My name is... just... The Pilgrim.

JEAN   Please begin.

INIGO   Bless me, Father, for I have sinned. It is well– several years since my last confession.

JEAN   Yes?

INIGO   Well, I am ashamed, Father Chanon.

JEAN   Shame for our sins can be a good starting point for change. But I am here to share God's forgiveness with you.

INIGO   But my sins are many, Father.

JEAN   Tell me.

INIGO   Seduction. Gambling. Vainglory. Pride. Anger. Rage. Ambition. Selfishness. Greed. Fighting in the street.

JEAN   I see. Go on.

INIGO   But you don't understand. I've seriously hurt people. Caused real damage.

JEAN   Go on.

INIGO *(struggling to breathe)* I have a feeling of revulsion, Father. I can't go through with this. *(He gets up and walks to the door)*

JEAN   Why not, Pilgrim?

INIGO   I am such a miserable creature. So low. So stained. So base and wicked.

JEAN   Tell me from the start.

INIGO   We'll be here for days, Father!

JEAN   So be it. Why not make it a written confession?

INIGO   No. I can't go through with this. Who am I fooling?

JEAN   Yourself.

INIGO   What?

JEAN   You're fooling yourself. You're allowing the bad spirit in you to sway you. To stop you from confessing.

INIGO   No. No. I'm just not good enough. I don't deserve to be forgiven, Father.

JEAN   No. You don't.

INIGO   Father?

JEAN   You don't deserve to be forgiven, Pilgrim.

INIGO   But –

JEAN   It's not about deserving. It's about mercy. God's mercy. And that's not given on a foundation of deserving. It's given as a gift. Freely. Whether we deserve it or not. It's all gift, Pilgrim.

INIGO   You don't know what I've done yet, Father Chanon.

JEAN   Whatever you've done. If you are truly sorry and determine to change, God will forgive you.

INIGO   No. No. This is just foolishness. I am what I am. Yes? I almost stabbed a Moor on the way here. Because he dishonoured our Lady. God's not going to forgive me. I've been deluding myself. What was I thinking?

INIGO sinks to the floor.

JEAN puts his hand on INIGO's shoulder.

Music. Monks chant. Lights fade.

Monk's beautiful plainchant is heard more loudly.

Lights fade up.

Three days later. INIGO is kneeling.

JEAN   And I absolve you from your sins in the name of the Father, and of the Son and of the Holy Spirit.

INIGO   Amen.

JEAN   Go in peace now.

INIGO   But have I told you everything?

JEAN *(smiling)* It took three days to write your confession, Pilgrim. You've told me everything.

INIGO   I hope there's nothing I've forgotten, though. Any detail. Any tiny detail. Perhaps I need to go over it again. In detail.

JEAN   No. Go in peace now.

INIGO   Ah. Yes. I feel so much... Thank you, good Father Chanon. Please take my mule for the service of the monks here at the monastery.

JEAN   If that's what you want.

INIGO   It is Father. *(Pause)* I have made a secret plan for God. I would like to tell you.

JEAN   Please.

INIGO   To walk barefoot to Jerusalem. Living on nothing but herbs. No money. Just trusting in God to provide. Like St Francis. And stay in the Holy Land. For ever.

JEAN   I bless you in this. *(He makes the sign of the cross)* May the Lord bless you and protect you on your camino.

INIGO   Well. Thank you, Father Chanon. *(He goes to the door)*

JEAN   Take this. *(He hands him a small book)*

INIGO   What is it?

JEAN   A book of spiritual exercises.

INIGO   What's that?

JEAN   A few exercises to keep you healthy. In the spirit. Keep you in good practice. Do them every day.

INIGO *(enthusiastic)* Like duelling exercises? I practise them every day. Religiously.

JEAN *(smiles)* Yes. These are a little less violent, perhaps. But the training of a spiritual warrior requires even more discipline, Pilgrim.

INIGO   Good. Thank you.

JEAN   They were written by our Abbot, Cisneros. Based on ideas and ways of prayer dating back to the Desert Fathers.

INIGO   Thank you, Father Chanon. I will practise them every day.

JEAN *(smiles)* Religiously?

INIGO *(smiles)* Yes. *(He goes to leave)*

JEAN   And Pilgrim.

INIGO   Yes?

JEAN   Go calmly now.

INIGO   Calmly?

JEAN   You'll see.

INIGO exits.

Lights fade.

CHAPEL OF THE BLACK MADONNA. MONTSERRAT. MARCH 24th 1522. NIGHT.

The statue of the Madonna of Montserrat is lit up by hundreds of candles. The sound of singing fills the air. The smoke of pungent incense.

INIGO, now in BEGGAR'S clothes, limps through the smoke and stands in front of the statue.

INIGO *(we hear his interior prayer)* Our Lady of Montserrat. Mother Mary – the mother that never leaves me. *(He removes his sword and dagger. Hangs them at the altar.)* Here are my most treasured possessions. My sword and dagger. I hang them as an offering to you. As a symbol of the renunciation of my former life. *(He holds his arms stretched out from his shoulders.)* I stand or kneel here before you all night as your poor knight. Accept my devotion which is offered to you in the spirit that Amadis De Gaul, that worthy knight and hero, may have offered to you.

From this moment, I offer no human lady my devotion and love. This is all now yours, most tender and loving and sweet Virgin Mary. Guide me in my new duels and adventures for your Son and lead me to the most glorious quests of goodness, kindness, fasting and the most extreme penitence and poverty.

Lights change. Passage of time.

Bell tolls six. Dawn.

INIGO stands with his arms still outstretched.

INIGO   Now I must leave for Barcelona to take ship on my pilgrimage to Jerusalem, My Lady. I will not go on the direct road as I may be recognised by people from my former life at Court and they will try to make much of me and tempt me back to my old dead, vainglorious ways. I will now be unable to make it on time for the required pilgrim's blessing from the Pope at Easter so will need to postpone for a year. I will find some back road and stay in a small town somewhere and live and work as a nameless Pilgrim in a hospice for a while. Bless me in this plan, my Mother. *(Crosses himself and leaves the church)*

Lights fade to:

CAVE. MANRESA. MARCH 1522

INIGO   Ah, this is it.

Damp, dark cave. I can hear the river outside. Cave. Excavate the dark, bright cave of my soul. (*He lies on the ground.)*

Lie down. Lie down on the cold stone. Feel the energy of the rock. The Earth. The Planet. Far from the judging eyes outside.

Ah, this feels right. This feels like the place.

A hermit. I will fast like those desert Fathers.

I will pray for seven hours a day. I will pray the exercises of Cisneros that Father Chanon gave me. I will make some notes of my own in my journal.

This is my... space. My palace. My castle. My Casa Grande. *(He is smiling. Deliriously happy)*

Lights fade.

We hear the other-worldly sound of monks chanting. Lights cross fade to:

JEAN CHANON'S CELL. MONTSERRAT.

JEAN and INIGO are in mid-conversation.

INIGO   Now I'm a nobody. Which is how I want it.

JEAN   But you have attracted attention. You now have crowds of followers in Manresa too. You are not formally educated in theology and yet you talk of God. This could raise suspicion.

INIGO   I only want to share my love of God. My joy. Everyone should feel this happy.

JEAN   Your naivety is touching, Pilgrim. But foolish. You must be aware of the prevailing wind. The political storm. This fear of heresy. The excommunication of Luther. Anyone giving cause for doubt is inviting danger. Be careful, Pilgrim.

INIGO   But I've never been political.

JEAN   We all are part of the political, Pilgrim. As Christ himself was. While there will always be God, there will still always be Caesar.

INIGO   Well I want nothing to do with Caesar. Ever again. All the crawling I saw at Court and fawning to power. Not for me. I will be a nameless pilgrim in the Holy Land. Trusting in God's providence and helping others. That's all I want. No-one will ever give me a second thought. Thank God.

JEAN   If that's what you desire.

INIGO   It is. More than anything. Father. I... I feel... such joy.

INIGO AT PRAYER IN HIS CELL. DOMINICAN MONASTERY. MANRESA 1522.

There is a big hole in one end, dug for structural work.

INIGO   O God. God. Where are you? Have you left me? *(A different voice seems to emerge from him)* "You! Look at you. Think you're special eh? What kind of life is this you're getting involved with? How are you going to keep it up 'til you're seventy? Look at you in your rags. Your pathetic mask wearing. Your stupid play-acting. What mask is it this time? The Lover? The Duelling Hidalgo? The Knight? Despairing Sick Man? The

Beggar? The Desert Father? Yes. Now it's the Monk. The Strict Ascetic.

And what if God doesn't even exist? What then? Be easy on yourself. Go back to Loyola. Have a good bath. Wash your lovely hair. Cut your filthy nails. Sleep in clean sheets." *(He forces voice away)* Shut up! Shut up! Shut. Up. You swine. Whoever you ae. Can you promise me even an hour of life? Just when I felt I was making progress. But I'm still the same old Inigo. *(He starts to pull at his rags and slap himself, shouting)* COME ON LORD! You're cruel, Lord. Cruel. COME ON! EVEN IF I HAVE TO WALK ON ALL FOURS AND FOLLOW A DOG TO GIVE ME THE CURE I'LL DO IT! I'LL DO IT! I have no pride left. I have nothing left. *(Pause)* I'm a failure. Everything I've tried I've failed at. Courtier, Soldier, Diplomat. Now deluding myself I can walk the spiritual path. Even this I fail at. I must just face it: my face doesn't fit. My face doesn't fit the bloody universe. Alright God. Alright universe. I finally get it. I'm not book-clever but I learned a lot from the blacksmith's children. And I'm a Basque, alright? I'm a country boy at heart and I can smell the change in the seasons. I can taste the snow in the air before it falls on our mountains. I can feel when the apple trees in our orchards are about to blossom. I can tell when the soil in a field will yield rich fruit. And I know when a field is barren, dead. I know when a tree is dead. And-this-tree-is. Dead. *(Pause)* Feel better. Good to have just accepted it. Feel nothing now. Just want it all to... stop now. *(He looks at the floor of the cell and the large crack or aperture with a deep drop in it)* This hole should do it. They've been digging it for weeks. *(He stands over the open hole)* So. An end to this failure called Inigo. This mask-wearing fraud. The black hole. Deep. Dark. And now. The final mask. Death. *(He is about to fall in)* Jesus! Help me! O God. God.

He falls prostrate on the floor.

Lights fade.

Sound of plainchant.

IN THE CELL OF THE BENEDICTINE MONK, JEAN CHANON. MONTSERRAT.

INIGO is kneeling. He is still in beggar's clothes.

JEAN   A spiritual practice is not only about joy and consolation. If you are serious about your soul these dark nights will come. This can be painful. And heroically hard work.

INIGO   But I was tempted to kill myself. I was within a breath of damnation.

JEAN   And you found the strength to fight it. It is an urge that you must fight against with all the strength you can. God will help you.

INIGO   Yes, Father. *(Beat)* I wanted to tell you of some things.

JEAN   Things, Pilgrim?

INIGO   Yes. Even if there were no scriptures to teach us about matters of faith I would be willing and happy to die for them. Just on the foundation of these things that have been revealed to me.

JEAN *(calm, smiling)* Go on.

INIGO   Well. I saw a light. From which God was creating light itself. The – essence of light. I'm not expressing this very well.

JEAN   Go on.

INIGO   And I know I don't have the words to explain this one. But one day I was going in my devotions to a church, a bit more than a mile from Manresa. It's called St. Paul's and I had to walk along by the Cardoner river. I sat down facing the river which ran deep below. As I stared into the river, feeling the sparkly clean water flushed through with sun, the whole thing came to me in an instant. It wasn't a vision as such but – all I can say is that the gates of my understanding were blown open and I understood about the nature of faith and scripture but also time and space... the natural world and learning and philosophy and... I saw everything in a new way.

As the river tumbled and rolled and sparkled I breathed in... the – stuff of life. The deep core of... meaning. I was looking out at the world and in at my interior landscape with new eyes. I was... let in on the secret of it all. I am – not just in my attire – or my outward mask... or my childish dreams of being the best... but a new man. With a new mind. A new man. For others. And everything... everything's changed. (*Pause*) See? I knew I wouldn't be able to put it into words properly.

JEAN (*stares at him for a while*) These are... these are wonderful insights, Pilgrim. Thank God for them. But they are not ends in themselves. Calmly see where they lead you.

INIGO   Yes, Father. I will. Thank you.

JEAN   Go in peace. And may God bless your pilgrimage to Jerusalem. Go well, Pilgrim.

INIGO   Thank you Father. (*Leaves*)

Lights fade.

Sound of church bells cut through.

Lights up.

OUTSIDE THE CHURCH OF SANTA MARIA DEL MAR. BARCELONA 1524.

A BEGGAR enters. Very bedraggled. He wears nothing on his body except "breeches of a shabby grey material that come down to his knees and leave his legs bare, a pair of old shoes, a black cloth jacket which doesn't fasten properly and is badly torn at the shoulders, and a short shabby coat."

We gradually see that it is INIGO, almost unrecognisable from before.

INIGO   Alms! Alms in the name of God.

A WOMAN in a veil has been watching him. She is very finely dressed.

WOMAN   It's God's work that I see you again.

INIGO   Again, Madam?

WOMAN   My name is Isabel Roser. You were here in Barcelona a few months ago. I saw you here outside Santa Maria del Mar. You were talking of God and I saw you give away all the money you had begged to those who had even less than you. Since then I've prayed for you every night.

INIGO   I'm glad you did, Madam Roser.

ISABEL   You look ill. Pale. Much more ragged than when I saw you before. Where have you been?

INIGO   Pilgrimage to Jerusalem. I wanted to stay. But it is dangerous for foreigners. I have no fear, but the Franciscans threatened me with excommunication if I didn't leave. So. God had other plans. For now. But I will return. I must. It's all I want. Then a rather perilous homeward voyage. Shipwrecks. Pirates. I have walked barefoot through lands at war, begging the whole way. I have been arrested. Interrogated. Tortured. But God has spared me. The Camino was... *(He just stares ahead, deeply moved, unable to express it)*

ISABEL   Do you have somewhere to stay? My husband and I would be honoured to have you stay with us. Our house is far too big for us. You are welcome.

INIGO   Thank you, Madam but the good Ines Pascual de Manresa has given me an attic in her Barcelona house.

ISABEL   An attic?

INIGO   It is all I requested. It is a palace after the streets and the fields. But I can make a fine bed of cobbles if need be, Madam.

ISABEL   May I ask your name?

INIGO   The Pilgrim.

ISABEL   Dine with us tonight, good Pilgrim.

INIGO (*thinks for a while*) No. Thank you, Madam Roser. But my bread and water will suffice.

Music as lights fade. Time lapse.

Lights up, several months later:

ISABEL'S HOUSE. BARCELONA 1525.

ISABEL talks with JERONIMO ARDEVOL, MASTER of Latin Grammar, INIGO'S teacher.

ISABEL   That – light. That light that shone from his face. This is the first truly holy man I've ever met. Our family has one of the best pews in the Cathedral, Master Ardevol. Intimate suppers with the Archbishop and the Cardinal. The Abbots of the Monasteries having fine dinners at our beautiful town house.

ARDEVOL   And there's Inigo. In his rags. Gratefully eating a scrap of bread. Smiling. Listening.

ISABEL   Yes. God, something needs to happen. The Church needs to get its hands dirty. To open the wooden door of the carpenter's workshop. To sit with the poor carpenter in the sawdust and learn to love. I'd been struggling with my faith. Not with God but some of the proud hombres that call themselves the clergy. Their fear of women. Their long, humourless faces. Their sidling away and their sneering, well-versed intellectual and social snobbery. I was hanging on to a cliff edge of faith. Of meaning. I was almost falling as my fingernails began to lose their grip. Then I met Inigo. He saved my faith. His humility. His love. Here was a man that loved my soul. Loved me. As I am. And his spiritual exercises...

ARDEVOL   Ah, yes.

ISABEL   They changed me. How did he know? How could he know how a woman feels deep in her heart? Men don't know these things. Pardon me, good Master Ardevol but men don't open up their hearts. Men don't weep with compassion and love. But he does. He talks of "feeling" the will of God. Feeling.

ARDEVOL   But he lives at such an intense pitch. I wish him more peace. And calm. He yearns for solitude and obscurity yet crowds beat a path to his attic door. But we must persuade him to get an education. To defend himself. Alcala University would be a good choice.

Optional dialogue follows:

[*INIGO enters.

INIGO   I'm sorry for calling unannounced. I was on my way to the convent.

ISABEL   You are welcome Inigo. Please sit down.

INIGO   Thank you Isabel. I've done my Latin Homework, Master Ardevol. Not much progress, I'm afraid.

ARDEVOL   But you are progressing Inigo.

INIGO   If so it is thanks to your expert tutelage, good Master Ardevol. But I still feel such a fool. I feel like such an idiot in a schoolroom with boys of five or six. God's really giving me a penance with this!

ARDEVOL   Yes. I fear you may never be a professor of Latin but you will acquire enough to gain admittance to university. Alcala would be a good choice. A vibrant, open-minded young university. Full of enthusiasm for Erasmus and the new culture. His *Enchiridion* is a lovely little book. About one's personal relationship with God.

INIGO   I don't really know his work. I've heard of him of course, but I'm not really any kind of academic.

ISABEL   Your own *Spiritual Exercises* are full of help to find one's personal relationship with God. The use of the imagination to put oneself actually in the Bible stories. To meet the divine deep in our imaginations. Our desires. Our souls. Face to face.

INIGO   Yes. Our imagination is one of the best places to find the divine in us.

ARDEVOL   Yet for the unqualified to talk in public of a personal relationship with God can be dangerous.

INIGO   I will just tell the truth.

ARDEVOL   That may not be enough. God wants you to stay alive. To do that now is to live by your wits. Learn the way the world of power speaks. Just like you're learning Latin.

INIGO   I know how earthly power works. From my time at Court. And I'm not interested, Master Ardevol.

ARDEVOL   But your message will go further.

INIGO   But at what cost? *(Pause)* To my soul?

ARDEVOL   Very well. But get some qualifications. Go to Alcala when you have finished your study here. Lectures on Logic from Dominic Soto, Natural Philosophy from Albert the Great, Theology from Peter the Lombard.

INIGO   But what about helping people? My mission? With the poor and in the hospices? My prayer life?

ISABEL   Dear Inigo you will be able to do all your work more openly.

INIGO   But a university course?

ISABEL   Inigo. Go to Alcala when you have finished your Latin grammar.

INIGO   I will reflect on this further.

ISABEL   You! Such a stubborn Basque.

INIGO   It is true. But I will examine this rigorously. I will use the *'Pro Contra'* decision making technique from the *Exercises*. I will draw up two columns for and against going to Alcala. Then two columns for and against not going. Then I will live a few days as if I had decided one way. Then the other. Then reflect deeply on how these choices make me feel. God wants for us what we want. So I should find what I desire. Really. And not the illusion. Or what I think I ought to want. *(Beat)* These are things I began to discern on my sickbed back home. But then, that is where everything began. Well. I must go. I have a meeting with the sisters at the convent.

ISABEL   Good. Be careful Inigo.

INIGO   Always. *(He bows and leaves)*

Optional dialogue ends within ARDEVOL's next line.

ARDEVOL   Careful indeed.*] People like our beloved Inigo are seen as trouble causers.

ISABEL   He is making powerful enemies.

ARDEVOL   Of course.

Lights fade.

A STREET. BARCELONA. NIGHT. 1525.

INIGO walks along in his threadbare clothes. A GENTLEMAN appears from the shadows.

GENTLEMAN   Are you the fellow known as Inigo? Working with nuns at the convent?

INIGO   Yes, Brother. How can I help you?

GENTLEMAN *(he takes out a thick wooden club and hits INIGO hard)* By minding your own business.

INIGO   How have I offended you, Brother?

GENTLEMAN There used to be a quiet, gentleman's agreement that the sisters were allowed gentlemen callers and a blind eye would be turned to it.

INIGO Yes, Brother and I've been talking to the sisters who –

GENTLEMAN Oh yes. You've been talking to them alright. Now my Theresa won't so much as give me a peck on the cheek. She says she's done some stupid exercises you gave her. Whole place was like a jolly good finishing school for ladies.

INIGO *(angry, tough. Gentleman recoils a bit in surprise)* A Holy Order is not a finishing school! Or a brothel. How dare you use it as such when it is a place of contemplation and prayer.

GENTLEMAN *(clubs him again)* Don't you lecture me. You're not even a priest. Just a filthy little jumped-up beggar.

INIGO *(trying to restrain his anger)* You're lucky I no longer bear arms sir.

GENTLEMAN Ha! Ha! Listen to it. There's plenty of very important people you and your followers have annoyed with your meddling, some of whom are priests and the occasional bishop and cardinal too.

INIGO *(now calmer)* They must be given the chance to change as well.

GENTLEMAN *(clubs him again)* Keep-your-nose-out. Understand? Just stop all this meddling and let's just keep things as they are, alright?

INIGO *(explodes into fury now. A loud, powerful voice. So much so that GENTLEMAN is dumbstruck)* As they are? As they are? Yes you'd like that wouldn't you? The status stinking quo. These convents are one of the few places where women can go to live a life of peace, of spirituality, without the crushing demands of conformity to a life that men decree. *(To himself, briefly)* Magdalena.

Isabel. Having their spirits stifled. *(To GENTLEMAN)* Oh yes! Let's keep things as they are, shall we? *(Beat, quieter now)* I know you sir. I've known men like you all too well. So go on. Beat me. Because as long as I have life in me I will do the Lord's work. And look at my eyes. *(GENTLEMAN does so. He is a bit scared now. Quiet. Still)* Can you see any fear of death? No fear. I have seen and heard my own bones crack and splinter in battle, sir. And I have put far better men than you to the sword. So. Go on. You'll have to kill me to stop me. I just wish it was at the hands of a real man.

GENTLEMAN Filthy beggar scum! *(The GENTLEMAN proceeds, unchallenged by INIGO, to brutally club him, leaving him for dead)* Do-gooding nuisance! Now go to hell, beggar. No-one'll miss you up here. *(He spits on the motionless body of INIGO. Runs off)*

Two young men come on. ARTEAGA and CALISTO, students at the university. They see INIGO. They touch him.

CALISTO Master Inigo. Master Inigo.

ARTEAGA That's it. They've actually killed him this time.

CALISTO Oh God no. At last we find someone we can believe in and they kill him.

ARTEAGA I knew something like this would happen.

CALISTO Let's take him to Madam Roser.

MADAM ROSER'S HOUSE.

The sound of people praying 'The Rosary' is heard as ISABEL ROSER and Master ARDEVOL watch as INIGO is carried in by CALISTO and ARTEAGA.

They surround him and pray the Hail Mary in a low chant. The tableau recalls Renaissance paintings of the Pieta with the mourning women.

All speak in hushed tones.

ISABEL I knew it.

ARDEVOL It was only a matter of time. Lord. Heal your servant Inigo.

ISABEL If it is your will Lord, heal him. If not, heal us. Amen.

CALISTO No-one else at the university speaks with his authority.

ARTEAGA He's caused a stir with all the students here. He's free and open and talks the truth.

CALISTO Students are good at spotting horse shite. So's our Master Inigo.

ARDEVOL The truth can kill you. Inigo, we told you to be careful.

ISABEL He's brave, Master Ardevol.

ARDEVOL He's addicted to risk, good Doña Isabel.

ISABEL Life is risk. Love is risk. Christ's whole life was risk. As is everyone's.

ARDEVOL Let us pray for him. And if he recovers he must go to Alcala. It's safer.

They resume the Rosary with ISABEL leading it. The chanting fades as:

Lights cross fade to a furnace glowing in the dark.

At the blacksmith's forge we see the BLACKSMITH smash his hammer. We hear the loud clanging. We see LITTLE BOY INIGO staring into the flames. MARIA (singing the Basque lullaby 'Loyolako Txikie'.) The last hammer blow of the BLACKSMITH coincides with:

Sound of a judge's hammer. Scene changes to:

ALCALA. A COURT ROOM. NOVEMBER 21ST 1526.

Vicar General FIGUEROA sits on a throne-like chair. The setting should be reminiscent of the earlier Corregidor trial scene of the younger INIGO.

INIGO, CALISTO and ARTEAGA stand in the dock in chains.

FIGUEROA   An investigation having been made here in Alcala and a process begun by the Inquisitors regarding your way of life, I am bound to inform you that the verdict of this hearing on this twenty-first day of November in the year of our Lord fifteen twenty-six is that no error could be found either doctrinally or indeed with your aforementioned way of life. Henceforth you may continue without any hindrance.

INIGO   Thanks, friend.

GUARD *(hard)* The accused will address the Archbishop of Toledo's assistant, Vicar General Figueroa, as Your Reverence.

INIGO   I call everyone friend. Or brother. Or comrade. As Christ did.

GUARD   Silence!

FIGUEROA   It's quite alright, Guard. Friend, brother. I've been called worse. So. You are free to go. Next!

INIGO   If I may say, friend.

FIGUEROA   Yes?

INIGO   I can't really see what good these inquisitions do.

FIGUEROA *(looks surprised)*   Really?

INIGO   And I'd like to know if these inquisitors have found any heresy in us? Insults, lies and hatred for my person are a welcome opportunity to grow in humility. But I will not have my loyalty and faith questioned. So. Officially. For the record. Are we heretics?

FIGUEROA   No. *(The accused are relieved. Tougher)* If they had found heresy, they'd have burnt you.

INIGO   And they'll burn you too if they find heresy in you.

CALISTO and ARTEAGA can't believe he's just said that. Nor can FIGUEROA.

GUARD   Silence. Silence.

FIGUEROA   No, good Guard. He's right. *(Wry smile)* So try to keep your heads down, eh? Next!

As the accused are led out, the focus changes to.

OUTSIDE JAIL. ALCALA. JUNE 1527

ISABEL ROSER waits outside. INIGO comes out with ARTEAGA and CALISTO.

ISABEL   Inigo. Amigos. That's three trials now, Inigo. Forty-two days in jail this time. I counted every one of them.

ARTEAGA   Dear Isabel. After Figueroa's second investigation I thought we might be left in peace. After the third I was scared as to what Figueroa's verdict might be.

ISABEL   Yes?

CALISTO   We were found not guilty of heresy this time too.

ISABEL   Good. Thank God. But Inigo, you could have been executed. Do you realise how close you were to losing your life this time? At least you are free now.

INIGO   Free? How can I be free if I can't do my work?

ISABEL   But you can't just disobey Figueroa, Inigo.

INIGO   Can't I?

ISABEL and INIGO move away to one side.

ISABEL   Inigo. God wants us to be helped through the channels of those who love us. And love you. Many important people were prepared to help you but you risked death instead. You are aware of what they do to people found guilty of heresy?

INIGO   Yes.

ISABEL   The burning to death. The cruel, lingering torture. The unimaginable agony.

INIGO   Yes.

ISABEL   Ha. So Christ-like, so merciful. Our compassionate church indeed.

INIGO   I am aware of this.

ISABEL   This is just folly. Another grand, heroic gesture.

INIGO   No. No. This is what my family have always done. It's the Loyola way. A favour here. A word in the right ear there. No. No more sweet words behind tapestries. No accommodation with power. It's how I was sprung from jail when I was a youth in Guipuzcoa. *(ARTEAGA and CALISTO look at each other, surprised)* This is a matter of honour. I will rely on God, madam. And God alone. Even if it means death.

ISABEL   You are impossible. This is just your Basque pride. This isn't about God's will – this is about your pride. The pride of Narcissus. The naive, stubborn pride of Inigo de Loyola. *(Pause)* So what now?

INIGO   We have prayed in jail these last few weeks using the *Exercises* and reflected on such an outcome. And we have made a determination we must leave Alcala. Now.

ISABEL   Leave? And go where?

INIGO   Salamanca. A fine university. Our little group deserves the best. And the ban won't be binding on us there. And I will pray. Pray as if everything depended on prayer. And work. Work as if all depended on human action alone. *(Beat. To boys)* I'll see you in Salamanca!

ARTEAGA AND CALISTO Salamanca! Goodbye Isabel. Goodbye Inigo.

ISABEL   Goodbye boys. *(ARTEAGA and CALISTO go)* So, that is it? You're very cold.

INIGO   Cold?

ISABEL   There's a shard of ice in your heart.

INIGO *(starts to stutter)* My heart... is hotter than a blacksmith's furnace, Isabel.

ISABEL   Really?

INIGO   But there are... parts of my heart...

ISABEL   You give so much to strangers. Little to those closest to you. Why do you hide?

INIGO   I do not hide.

ISABEL   You hide. You are the most... elusive of men. A brief glimpse. Then you're gone. You say you run from no-one. Why then do you flee... from intimacy?

INIGO   There are certain intimacies... I will never taste again.

ISABEL   Where is all this leading, Inigo?

INIGO   I still yearn to go back to the Holy Land. With so many qualifications they will not send me back a second time.

ISABEL   What about comfort? The balm of friendship... the touch of a loved one.

INIGO *(starts to weep)* Yes. Yes. But I know such... such joy too. And disordered attachments can lead to illusion and more suffering.

ISABEL   Disordered attachments?

INIGO   Yes.

ISABEL *(weeps too)* Am I being selfish? Wanting you here? Yes. Yes.

INIGO   No, not selfish, Isabel.

ISABEL   Inigo.

INIGO   We will never be parted. Mere distance can never separate those whose souls God has forged together.

ISABEL   Perhaps.

INIGO   You and I, Isabel. Here and in heaven. Be brave.

ISABEL   Brave? What does that mean? Really. *(Pause)* So. Salamanca. You'd better go, Inigo.

Lights fade.

The BLACKSMITH smashes his hammer in the forge. LITTLE BOY INIGO watches the flames. The last hammer blow coincides with a JUDGE'S HAMMER as we cross fade to:

A COURT ROOM. SALAMANCA. 1527.

INIGO, ARTEAGA and CALISTO in chains.

CLERK   The Salamanca hearing is now in process. Be upstanding for the Vicar General Figueroa.

FIGUEROA *(entering)* Ah, so here we have him. Again. The one who's been making all the fuss. All this fuss over such a little man, eh, Loyola?

INIGO   Yes.

FIGUEROA   Yes what?

INIGO   Your Reverence.

FIGUEROA   Better. I know you people don't give a fig for authority but you will comport yourself with dignity this time, Loyola. And be truthful. Your life may depend on it. You do understand that, Loyola?

INIGO   Yes, your Reverence.

FIGUEROA   Do you swear on this Bible that the evidence you give shall be the truth in God's name?

CLERK holds out Bible.

INIGO   I so swear. In God's name.

FIGUEROA *(takes out a copy of the 'Exercises'.)* Interesting little book this. Your *'Spiritual Exercises'*. However obscure the authorial provenance.

INIGO   Your Reverence?

FIGUEROA   Did you write it?

INIGO   Yes, your Reverence.

FIGUEROA   Interesting. Hardly original though, is it? Just a lot of re-heated stuff from the Desert Fathers by way of Cisneros. Correct?

INIGO   I was hugely indebted to them, your Reverence. I have added some suggestions myself.

FIGUEROA   Yes. So you have. What gives you the right, an uneducated beggar, to interpret the Bible?

INIGO   I'm just trying to help people, your Reverence.

FIGUEROA *(pause)* What make you of *Enchiridion* by Erasmus? Would you agree that the Erasmian tendency to alternate consideration of God's gifts with the recollection of suffering consequent on sin is partly the result of a neo-platonic principle of spirituality?

INIGO   No.

FIGUEROA   Why?

INIGO   Because I didn't understand what you just said.

FIGUEROA   Really?

INIGO   I prefer the *Imitation of Christ* by A Kempis.

FIGUEROA   Why?

INIGO   It's simpler. More practical. Erasmus praises radical poverty, but I don't see him practising it himself. While Erasmus has many good qualities, I am more influenced by other, genuine radicals.

FIGUEROA   Are you prepared to give us names, Loyola?

INIGO   Yes, Your Reverence.

FIGUEROA   Good Loyola. This is better. Name them.

INIGO   Saint Francis of Assisi and Saint Dominic.

FIGUEROA   Ah. So. You expect me to believe any of that? The spirit of Erasmus runs through your scribblings, Loyola.

INIGO   Does it, Your Reverence?

FIGUEROA   Well, yes it does, Loyola. This emphasis upon a personal relationship with God.

INIGO   Yes, your Reverence?

FIGUEROA   That is what you're advocating then?

INIGO   Yes, your Reverence. But... but...

FIGUEROA *(to NOTARY)* You have that? *(NOTARY nods)* I thought as much. *(Pause)* I trust you have heard of the 'Alumbrados'?

INIGO   Yes, your Reverence.

FIGUEROA   Or the 'Illuminated'?

INIGO   Yes, your Reverence.

FIGUEROA   Would you count yourself among their number, Loyola?

INIGO   No, your Reverence.

FIGUEROA   Then how do you explain witness reports regarding the use of the word "illumination" and "illuminated" with reference to you and your followers?

INIGO   Well – I don't – really.

FIGUEROA   By what could a soul be illuminated directly?

INIGO *(starts to stutter)* I do not know.

FIGUEROA   Illuminated by what?

INIGO   I don't –

FIGUEROA   Illuminated by what?

INIGO   It sounds like –

FIGUEROA   Illuminated by what, Loyola?

INIGO   The Holy Spirit? *(Pause)*

FIGUEROA *(calm again)* Ah. There it is. You have just concurred with the Alumbrados and their heretical position.

INIGO   But I'm not saying –

FIGUEROA   Silence! I think you mean well Loyola. But you and your kind are a menace. A real danger to souls. Unwittingly perhaps. But a danger nevertheless. So why not just drop this nonsense? Why risk public humiliation and death?

INIGO   I am a loyal servant of the Church, your Reverence. If there is heresy in anything I have done then charge me with it.

FIGUEROA *(pause)* What is it, eh, Loyola? What are you up to, eh? A Basque gentleman of the very minor nobility. Love your masks, don't you? Which one is it today? The Errant Knight? The Soldier? The Beggar? The Holy Man? The Religious Leader? Which mask are you wearing today, eh, Loyola? Do you actually know who the real you is? *(Comes right up close. Face to face with INIGO. Quiet)* I'm watching you, Loyola. I can spot a fake fifty leagues away. *(He sweeps off, followed by NOTARY. As he goes)* Confined to cells. Pending verdict.

Lights fade.

End of act one.

ACT TWO

We see and hear the BLACKSMITH smash his hammer in the foundry.

Scene changes to:

PARIS. TWO YEARS LATER. ST BARBE COLLEGE. PARIS UNIVERSITY. 1529.

INIGO's room. Very run down and cramped. Poverty.

INIGO is talking to a roommate, PETER FAVRE, a sensitive, angelic looking young man.

FAVRE   Now it's all so clear, good Inigo.

INIGO   I'm glad, Favre.

FAVRE   These miraculous *Exercises*. No wonder everyone at the university is talking about them. You must be a genius, Inigo. How did you come up with them?

INIGO   Calm down, Peter! Let's just say I had a lot of help.

FAVRE   I'm glad you did. And I'm glad they found you not guilty in Salamanca. Why would anyone want to punish you, dear Inigo? My life. From the hillsides of Savoy tending my sheep as a little boy and crying in my longing for an education. Playing a game of 'Priests' with my friends. Then here. The bustle of Paris. Fear. Confusion. Should I be a doctor? Lawyer? Teacher. Now I know. The *Exercises* have helped me to see: I will be ordained a priest.

INIGO   If that's what you genuinely desire.

FAVRE   Oh yes. Thank you, Inigo.

The door opens. In comes a handsome strong young man, glowing with health.

YOUNG MAN   Hello Favre. So. This the new room-mate? I know we're broke but you can't expect three of us to share this cupboard!

FAVRE   Inigo. This is my friend, Francisco.

INIGO   Good to meet you, Francisco.

FRANCISCO   Oh yes. I've heard all about you. The Old Man. Well as long as you don't snore, don't fart and keep your sanctimonious ideas to yourself and let me lead my life, we'll be fine. I'll be out exercising most of the time anyway so you won't see much of me.

INIGO   Exercising?

FAVRE   Francisco is one of the best athletes of Paris University.

FRANCISCO   No Peter. That's not quite true. I've won all the golden medallions since I've been here. I'm just the best.

FAVRE   And the most modest.

INIGO (*staring at him intently, smiling*) Congratulations Francisco.

FRANCISCO   That's Don Francisco de Jassu y Xavier to you.

INIGO   Xavier? Not from Castle Xavier in Najera?

XAVIER   That's Navarre to you.

INIGO   I fought at the battle of Pamplona for the Duke of Najera.

XAVIER   Hardly a battle. A skirmish perhaps. Don't look much like a soldier.

INIGO   I was never a regular soldier as such. I was wounded.

XAVIER   Too bad. My family were on the other side.

INIGO   Oh.

XAVIER   My brothers fought at Pamplona. Perhaps one of them wounded you.

INIGO Perhaps.

XAVIER O well. At least you're a Basque. Where are you from?

INIGO Loyola. Near Azpeitia. Guipuzcoa.

XAVIER Oh. Yes. But my family were of the old nobility. My father was the President of the Royal Council of Navarre. 'Til your Duke replaced him. He died of grief.

INIGO I'm so sorry, Francisco.

XAVIER Don't be. I don't need your sympathy.

FAVRE You must let him give you the *Exercises*, Francisco.

XAVIER Oh yes. These *Exercises* everyone's talking about. Sorry. No time. Any pious stuff and you're out. Peter's the only holy type I have any time for. Because he's not a religious hypocrite and he's my friend. *(Beat)* You see them. All the Holy Joes. Coming out of the College chapel. Far too holy to smile. Kicking mud in the beggar's face outside. Bastards. And besides. I've got something I need to get on with. It's called my life. *(He dumps his bags)*

INIGO I can help you.

XAVIER Oh. Here we go. Hallelujah brother!

INIGO No. I can help you find work. Here at the university.

FAVRE Listen to him, Francisco. He helps all who ask him. He can find you work here.

XAVIER Very well. Don't mind that kind of help. Thanks. O well. I'm off. Got a meeting with a very lovely lady. Bye! *(He exits)*

FAVRE Sorry, Inigo.

A knock on the door. FAVRE runs to it.

FAVRE Francisco if that's you coming back to apologise for being rude, its too late!

Opens door. In it stands a charismatic man in the impressive clerical garb of a bishop. It is GIAN PIETRO CARAFA.

FAVRE   Oh. Can I help you Father?

CARAFA   It's "Bishop". Carafa.

FAVRE   Sorry. Bishop. Please come in. *(Dusts down a rickety old chair)* Do sit down.

CARAFA does so. His rich robes find contrast with the shabbiness of the room.

CARAFA   Which one of you is the man known as Inigo?

INIGO   That is I, friend.

CARAFA   Friend?

INIGO   I hope you are?

CARAFA   My title is Bishop Gian Pietro Carafa.

INIGO   Yes, friend.

CARAFA   Still you do not afford me the courtesy of employing my title.

INIGO   We are all equal in the eyes of God and I love all and respect all equally, dear brother.

CARAFA   Respect is due, if not for my person, then for my office and it would bode well for you to learn humility. The root of all virtues.

INIGO   Yes.

CARAFA   May we speak alone?

FAVRE   Yes. Well. Yes, of course. *(Exits)*

CARAFA *(looks around the room)* Well. I see you practise what you preach.

INIGO   Preach?

CARAFA   Poverty.

INIGO   I don't exactly preach. Just share my thoughts with equals about God. *(CARAFA stares at*

INIGO.) To what do I owe this unexpected honour of your visit, comrade?

CARAFA   I'm returning to Rome after business in Paris. I've heard you've had a few brushes with the Inquisition, Loyola. Alcala. Salamanca. Now here in Paris. Not on the run, are we?

INIGO   No. I was acquitted in all those places. I came to Paris for the university.

CARAFA   I have heard some of the things you've been saying about myself and my order, the Theatines.

INIGO   What have I been saying, friend?

CARAFA   That I live a life of luxury and my original ideals of poverty for my order have been corrupted by that life of luxury.

INIGO   Good brother, the work you have done with your order is of God.

CARAFA   Good of you to say so.

INIGO   Nevertheless, one may bear in mind the saintly ones like Saint Francis or Saint Dominic and how they conducted themselves when they founded their orders by their good example. They didn't live any more comfortably than their brothers.

CARAFA *(sudden anger)* How dare you? How dare you sit in judgement upon me?

INIGO   I do not judge anyone, friend.

CARAFA   I have renounced my ecclesiastical privileges to be at the forefront of the reform movement. I accepted office and promotion and a small degree of influence within the Church to strengthen the good work with the sick and poor that my order performs. And performs rather well, due to God's grace. This is a paradox but one I feel you can grasp. To use earthly powers in order to help the needy and the weak. I do not seek advancement for my own vainglory, Loyola.

INIGO　　　　Dear friend. You are a celebrated and worthy servant of God. I will never have an order. Perhaps it may please God for me and a few friends to live simple lives of poverty in the Holy Land. This is my dream. Or to join a corrupt, existing order and change it from within. But if I did have an order as such – seems strange even putting it hypothetically – it would be radically different.

CARAFA　　　　Oh yes?

INIGO　　　　I would hope that none of us would take official office. No bishops. No cardinals. No rules. No regulations.

CARAFA　　　　Why not?

INIGO　　　　There is too much temptation in the corridors of Rome. Office. Titles. Structures. Power. Influence. For me, anyway. But not for one as strong as yourself, Gian.

CARAFA　　　　Corrupt orders? Temptation in Rome? Dangerous talk, Loyola.

INIGO　　　　Dangerous?

CARAFA (*suddenly his submerged anger surfaces again*) You took the student Diego away from my order, Loyola.

INIGO　　　　Ah.

CARAFA　　　　One of the most brilliant candidates I ever had. You seduced him away from the Theatines.

INIGO　　　　Brother Diego is a fine student as you say. I gave him the *Exercises* and he wanted to join our little group of friends.

CARAFA　　　　I can see right through you, Loyola. I know your little game. This *faux naiveté*. But beneath that mask of sanctity is a schemer, a manipulator with more worldly ambition than ever I could dream of. I know my calling. I am following my Lord. And for me that's just a bit more complex than being a naive street evangelist.

I am adult enough to embrace the contradictions of the real world. Look at you. Not even ordained and lecturing me on moral rectitude. You Spaniards are all the same. Scheming. Dangerous. Arrogant.

INIGO But I'm not a Spaniard. I'm a proud Basque, Gian.

CARAFA Don't Gian me. It's Bishop Carafa to you, student. Bishop. For now. Basque, Spaniard: you're all the same. *(Pause. He goes for calm)* God knows what is in my heart. And I can live with that.

INIGO Good. I'm pleased for you.

CARAFA *(gets up, smiles)* You and your big show of poverty. Keep your eyes open, Spaniard.

INIGO Thank you, dear friend. And Gian. Don't be afraid.

CARAFA Afraid?

INIGO Of anything. Especially not of me. I'm no-one.

CARAFA looks at INIGO, very unsettled now. He leaves. FAVRE comes back in.

FAVRE He seemed a cheery soul.

INIGO Yes. Our Italian friend is very angry with me.

FAVRE Not a good enemy to have, Inigo.

Lights fade.

INIGO'S ROOM, PARIS UNIVERSITY. MONTHS LATER.

FRANCISCO XAVIER is in mid-argument with PETER FAVRE and INIGO.

FAVRE So you admit these *Exercises* work Xavier?

XAVIER Work Favre? Work? That's not the point.

FAVRE   But you said –

XAVIER   Yes, I know.

FAVRE   What's the problem?

XAVIER   I wish I'd never met you, Inigo. You're a nuisance and a trouble causer.

FAVRE   He's a very spiritual man. A good man.

XAVIER   I know. I know, alright.

FAVRE   You're not making much sense, Xavier.

XAVIER (*angry*) That's right! I'm not making any sense. That's the problem. I wish I'd never made the *Exercises*. "You're supposed to be a scholar," you said. "I thought you had an open mind," you said. So I did. Just to get some peace. Then all this madness started happening. They started as thoughts. Imaginings. Now look at me. Giving away my things. Begging in the bloody street with you and the Companions. Visiting people in the Hospice. Praying. *Me*. Praying, Favre! I'm like the kind of idiot I used to mock. Quite wittily mock too. Used to enjoy baiting you two. I DON'T WANT THIS! I DON'T WANT TO BE ALL HOLY! I just wanted to get my degree. Restore my family's nobility. Make a tidy fortune and trumpet the name of Francisco Xavier with glory around the world. Now I just – I HATE THIS! – Now I just want to – to give it all up. Help others. Put others first. IT'S A LIVING NIGHTMARE! It's as if I'm someone else. One of my well-connected friends saw me begging in the street. He'll tell everyone. The shame. It's as if I'm in a dream and watching myself at a carnival ball trying on the mask of 'The Holy Man' and not being able to take it off! THIS IS THE TROUBLE WITH TAKING THE SPIRITUAL LIFE TOO SERIOUSLY! It's bloody inconvenient. And it ruins your social life. All my fashionable friends think I'm deranged now. So no more invitations to smart parties. No more moonlight liaisons with beauties on the banks of the Seine.

(Beat) And you know what the worst thing is? Eh? The really strange thing? I don't miss any of it. How is that possible? Eh? In fact I look at those people now and I just feel – compassion. And – don't tell anyone – but I pray for them. Yes. Me. I pray. So thanks, Favre. Thanks, Loyola. Thanks a lot for ruining my life. You have to admit, though: I put up a bloody good fight.

INIGO   Of course you did. You're a Basque. It was a long siege! I expected nothing less.

XAVIER   If only my brothers had aimed that cannonball properly at Pamplona. Just a few feet higher and I'd be a free man.

INIGO *(smiles, gently, teasing)* "The Lord works in mysterious–"

XAVIER   I'm warning you!

INIGO   You've been the hardest dough I've ever had to knead, Xavier.

XAVIER   Yes, and now look at me. Toast!

MAN'S VOICE *(offstage) Inigo... Inigo... Inigo!*

INIGO, FAVRE AND FRANCISCO Bobadilla.

The door flies open. A bearded, big ruddy-faced man bursts through the door.

MAN   Inigo! Inigo! That's it! I've done 'em. Your lovely, loco *Exercises.* You mad genius, come here! *(He goes up and roughly bear-hugs INIGO. Then the MAN plants a kiss on both his cheeks)* I love this man!

FAVRE   Calm down, Bobadilla.

BOBADILLA   How can I calm down?! I've just had my head blown off! My mad Castillian's bull's heart is pumping almost indecently with the love of God. And this little darlin'– *(He kisses INIGO again)*

INIGO   Please, Bobadilla.

FAVRE   Bobadilla. Look. He's a Basque. Bit reserved? Hugging and kissing – you know –

BOBADILLA *(draws his sword)* What are you saying, Savoyard? Come on then. Let's have you!

INIGO *(smiling)* Calm. Calm, Bobadilla.

BOBADILLA *(sheathes sword)* I'm sorry. It's just – oh I don't know. Ever since I came here from me little one horse town – but don't get me wrong – I've befriended several people *con muchas sustancia* – important people, here in Paris – I can hold me own with you noble boys. Not you, Favre. I know yer only a poor shepherd boy. Unlike you, at least we just about had a pot to piss in. But anyway. Where was I? Oh yes. Ever since I came here to Paris – this cold, miserable city – I've been slaving away at my studies – brilliantly, mind you – I'm always top of my class – Plato, Aristotle, Aquinas and in any language you want – Greek, Hebrew, Latin. Even French. Well– maybe not English. Yes, but who would? Where was I? Sorry – me mind's on fire. Oh, yes. So after all these weighty academic tomes there's Inigo's tiny little homemade notebook. Didn't look much. *(Beat)* Bang! Right between the eyes. That's it! What do we do? When can we get in there: healing, helping, saving? Come on! Let's get out there, men. Let's do it!

XAVIER *(deadpan)* Yes, but did the *Exercises* make an impression on you?

BOBADILLA *(smiles)* Not really.

XAVIER   No. Me neither. *(Beat)* They're dangerous alright. Ruin lives.

Lights fade.

INIGO'S ROOM. LATER.

A man named HERNANDEZ sits with INIGO.

INIGO   Is there anything I can do to help you, Signor Hernandez?

HERNANDEZ *(calm)* No. No. My life is over. I have nothing left to live for. Just the thought of another year fills me with horror.

INIGO   Please. I am well acquainted with melancholy, friend. Please allow me to help you.

HERNANDEZ Do not worry, Inigo.

INIGO   Well...

HERNANDEZ Well... perhaps... Do you dance?

INIGO   Dance?

HERNANDEZ Yes. One of your wonderful Basque dances. You Basques were born singing and dancing.

INIGO   I loved dancing. Many years ago. But −

HERNANDEZ I was in your homeland once. A happy time. Perhaps if I saw one of your joyous Basque dances again −

INIGO   Yes − but not from me, I'm afraid.

HERNANDEZ Please.

INIGO   No. Absolutely not. I am sorry.

HERNANDEZ You asked if there was anything you could do. Well. This could be it.

INIGO   You ask too much of me. It is no longer my humour. Dancing. I am far too − too...

HERNANDEZ I understand. I should go now.

INIGO   No, Signor Hernandez. Wait.

INIGO reluctantly gets to his feet. Slowly he forces himself to dance. This is a mortifying experience for him. He hums a Basque folk song to himself as he starts, hesitantly. He gradually throws himself intently into the dance, despite his limping leg. We see a glimpse of the wildness, intensity and passion of his youth again. He finishes with a flourish. He then reverts immediately to his reserved former self.

HERNANDEZ *(stands up, clapping)* Thank you. Thank you, dear Inigo. This is the first time I have smiled in months.

INIGO   I am happy for you, brother. *(Quiet)* But please. Never, ever ask me to do that again. And please. Tell no one.

Lights fade.

Lights up on:

INIGO'S ROOM. PARIS 1534.

INIGO is giving the 'Exercises' to ISABEL ROSER.

ISABEL   This is my favourite spiritual exercise. The imaginative contemplation.

The marked line is unnecessary repetition if the earlier Ardevol scene is played is its entirety.

INIGO   [*The imagination is one of the best places to find the divine within us.*] So, in your imaginative contemplation, how did you feel when you talked to Our Lady?

ISABEL   Light. Happy. As usual.

INIGO   Good. I like the way you imagined the scene so clearly. I have a final point.

ISABEL   Yes?

INIGO   The Bible text you placed yourself in, imaginatively. It's a wedding celebration.

ISABEL   Yes.

INIGO   In Cana.

ISABEL   Yes.

INIGO   Your organisational ability was as strong as ever.

ISABEL   Thank you.

INIGO   You showed the servants where to find the jars for the water and wine. You arranged the banqueting plan for the guests. You advised on the food. The choice of music.

ISABEL   Yes.

INIGO   Do you see?

ISABEL   Not quite.

INIGO   Perhaps you should be thinking about yourself a bit more? Your own needs. Your own soul and its progress.

ISABEL   Yes. I was just taking over their wedding, wasn't I?

INIGO   Well... *(They both start laughing)*

ISABEL   Yes. Yes. It seems so obvious when you put it like that. All these activities of mine may be taking my eye off what is most needful. I see. Good. *(Beat)* These *Exercises* are very popular back home in Barcelona. The number of Iniguistas – men and women – keeps growing. And believe it or not I give the *Exercises* to people.

INIGO   You have a great gift for it, Isabel.

ISABEL   Thank you. *(Beat)* So. Tell me. How are things here in Paris? How is your health, Inigo?

INIGO   I still suffer agony with my gallstones. Due to the extremity of my penances.

ISABEL   In secret I suppose?

INIGO   Yes.

ISABEL   Why?

INIGO   To train my soul. *(He falls to the floor in pain. She goes to him and comforts him)*

INIGO   Ah. *(She holds him)*

ISABEL   There Inigo. *(She hums a lullaby, strokes his head)*

INIGO   Ah, mother. Mother. *(She gradually helps him back into the chair)*

ISABEL   Any better?

INIGO   Yes. Yes. The wave has gone.

Pause.

ISABEL *(gently)* I wonder if you should discern whether these extreme penances may be what you call a disordered attachment.

INIGO   An attachment?

ISABEL   To an idea of suffering.

INIGO   Yes. Yes I will look into this.

ISABEL   I just wonder whether one day you may find that God might not require us to suffer unnecessarily? Whom are you seeking to please with it?

INIGO   Yes. Thank you Isabel. I will reflect on this. I will.

ISABEL *(smiling)* Your lovely hair. You lost most of it. Ahh.

INIGO   I know. It was a lovely head of hair too.

ISABEL   Ah. The Loyola modesty!

INIGO   I'm just stating the truth. *(They laugh)*

ISABEL   So. Your news.

INIGO   I feel I now have a group of lasting companions. Peter Favre, Francisco Xavier, Nicolas Bobadilla, Lainez and Salmeron, and the Portuguese, Rodrigues. My earlier followers and others fell away.

ISABEL   So. Is this the birth of an order?

INIGO   We do not want to found an order. And we have no leader. We are just a group of free equals, companions who want to work for the common good. All we own will be shared equally. All our decisions are made together by majority vote. We have made a determination that this should be our collective way of proceeding.

ISABEL   Determination. I know what that word means to you!

INIGO   We have contemplated deeply using the *Exercises* and made a group discernment. After the conclusion of our studies, we will serve God in complete poverty and chastity, then live and work for the good of others in the Holy Land.

ISABEL   What if you should not be able to gain permission to stay in Jerusalem?

INIGO   In the unlikely event of that happening, we discerned that we should then go to Rome and see what is wanted of us there. *(Beat)* So, on the Feast of the Assumption, August 15th, 1534, our little group of Companions, *Companeros*, made our way to a little chapel outside Paris. St. Denis on Montmartre.

CHAPEL AT MONTMARTRE

We see on one side of the stage the group walking into the Chapel at Montmartre, FAVRE, XAVIER, BOBADILLA, LAINEZ, SALMERON, RODRIGUES. This action continues wordlessly – i.e. Once they have filed in, they kneel and FAVRE blesses them.

INIGO   We all made our vows. Favre, having recently been ordained, and being the only priest among us, said the Mass. We were a little group of equals dedicated to the love of our fellow men and women. This was a special moment for us. And for me. I've been brought so far. From it all being about me, and being the best, to it all being about others. From my childish illusions of greater glory for me, even after my conversion. Yes. I am still the same person. But I now realise that my past weaknesses have been refined, re-forged into strengths. So it's now evolved through years of study and discernment into *Ad Majorem Dei Gloriam*: To the Greater Glory of God.

INIGO 'steps out' of this scene and joins the group here, and we are left with a beautiful Renaissance chiaroscuro image of the dimly lit chapel and the group kneeling.

The BLACKSMITH smashes his hammer in the forge.

CHAPEL. LA STORTA. THREE YEARS LATER. AUTUMN 1537.

INIGO   This chapel. La Storta. The road to Rome. So, Lord. You seem to be leading us to Rome. But you know my dearest dream is to serve you in simplicity and anonymity in Jerusalem. *(He sees something)* Lord. Lord. Our Father. Is that you? Yes. And now you speak. "I will... be... favourable... to you... in Rome." I see You too now Jesus. I see You carry Your cross. *(Pause)* Jesus speaks to me now. "It is My will that you serve us". *(Weeps)* And now the tears. These welcome floods of joyful tears whenever you are near. Me, the tough, hard-nosed Basque. *(Laughs, then listens. Conversational)* Yes, brother. My friend. Ha ha. Yes. I know. Alright. Yes, I can be very stupid sometimes. Very slow. You're like a patient schoolmaster with a schoolboy. Thank you. But for now, Rome it is! *(Beat)* But what is this I feel now? Why do I see closed windows and doors?

Lights fade.

ROME. CARDINAL'S RESIDENCE. 1538.

CARAFA, now dressed in the crimson robes of a cardinal, and his nephew, CARLO CARAFA, a cleric.

CARAFA   So here they are. They're fanatics. We've just had the coldest winter on record in Rome and they go out in blizzards. They've only just arrived and they've founded a refuge for prostitutes, work round the clock in hospitals, preach in Santa Maria della Strada and in the streets, feed the hungry. And there's only a handful of them. What are they up to?

CARLO   It's just showing off, Uncle. I mean your Eminence, Cardinal Carafa.

CARAFA   Yes. Yes it is, Carlo. They've just barged their way in here with their boorish Spanish manners and their vulgar ostentatious piety.

CARLO   They haven't won many friends either with their 'Roman College'. I walked past the sign today "School of Grammar, Humanities and Christian Doctrine. Free."

CARAFA   Yes. That's the bit I can't understand. "Free."

CARLO   Well, he has many benefactors.

CARAFA   Yes. But still – how can he afford to run a school for free?

CARLO   Now he's attracting students away from other schools. Other orders. Like yours, Uncle. He's not making himself very popular.

CARAFA   Good. The Loyola mask is beginning to slip. He's unorthodox. And a dangerous radical. He's an Erasmian and an Illuminist. Despite his lies to the contrary.

CARLO   But he's never been found guilty of heterodoxy. He's been hauled in front of the Inquisition seven times now and they've found nothing.

CARAFA   It's only a matter of time. He's a fraud. This isn't personal, Carlo. He'll lead countless people to damnation. That's why it's our duty to stop him.

CARLO   Indeed, Uncle.

CARAFA   So how's your dossier on him progressing?

CARLO   Very well. Several powerful pieces of information are being strongly insinuated in certain influential ears.

CARAFA   Good. But I want no dirty tricks. The truth will be enough to protect innocent souls from this heretic.

CARLO   Yes, Uncle. I have shared our concerns with powerful allies in the curia regarding his crypto-Lutheranism.

CARAFA   Good.

CARLO   And our conviction that Loyola and his followers are Protean. Shape-shifters. Power-hungry.

CARAFA   Good. Good. So they are.

CARLO   And that they don't care what means they employ as long as their ends are achieved. That one's taking hold very well indeed.

CARAFA   Excellent. Merely the truth.

CARLO   This Loyola is hugely unimpressive. We shall swat him like a fly.

CARAFA   Oh do shut up, nephew.

CARLO   Pardon?

CARAFA   You're so ignorant you can't even see the sheer – You're not fit to untie his sandals.

CARLO   But Uncle –

CARAFA   He may be dangerously deluded but I still have enough of my soul alive to see what he is. You've never suffered, Carlo. Not like him. Or me. Once. For you it's always been a career. But for him. And me – once. It was a great calling. A mission. Yes. To truly burn with the love of one's fellow man. To carry the light of God to the poor, the dispossessed, the broken. To wipe away the tears of the suffering. To be the face, eyes, mouth, hands and fingers of Christ. And that's what he is. And I was – once. *(Pause)* I too was a radical reformer. I really felt I could be counted in the communion of saints one day. I felt such love. And compassion. Once – *(Looks around palace)* And now this. How did I get here, Carlo?

When did all this happen? He's stuck to his path. And I...
(Pause) I must destroy him.

Lights fade.

ROME. THE COMPANIONS' HOUSE. 1538.

The COMPANIONS are in mid-argument. INIGO remains calm.

BOBADILLA   What is the matter with these idiots?

XAVIER   Just calm down, Bobadilla.

BOBADILLA   No, Xavier. I'm sick of it.

XAVIER   We all are.

FAVRE   We must just keep on doing the Lord's will. In a calm, steadfast way.

BOBADILLA   Inigo! Come on. We can't just take all these lies about us on the chin. Just because you had the balls – pardon me – but the guts to take on that crypto-heretic Fra Agostino he's got his influential pals to try to rip us apart. Spaniards too.

XAVIER   And now people are openly calling you a crypto-Lutheran, Inigo.

BOBADILLA   Welcome to Rome!

INIGO   Truly, this year is full of the strongest attacks and persecution I have ever had to face in my life.

BOBADILLA   Why can't they just keep their noses out of our business?

FAVRE   We've done such good work here. Founded the Roman College, worked with the sick and the poor.

XAVIER   But if God wants us to suffer then we must embrace it. I'll suffer to the death if necessary if it be God's will.

BOBADILLA   That's rubbish, Xavier. God wants us to live and do good here on earth, man.

XAVIER   You've got a good heart, Bobadilla. But a big mouth, which I'm happy to shut for you.

BOBADILLA   Come on then!

FAVRE   Stop it you two.

INIGO   We are under attack. From several powerful sources.

BOBADILLA   Yes. Yes. I'm sorry Xavier. Me and my big mouth.

XAVIER   It's alright. You big Castillian bull.

BOBADILLA   Watch it, you Basque mule. Sorry.

INIGO   We have a fight on our hands. And we must give it our all. Our fullest, most mindful attention.

BOBADILLA   We'll need a miracle.

INIGO   Yes. We will pray. As if everything depended on prayer.

BOBADILLA   And act –

XAVIER   As if everything depended on our actions alone. As you have taught us.

INIGO   Yes.

XAVIER   But there is so much opposition to us now, Inigo.

BOBADILLA   All the lies are having an effect.

FAVRE   Children no longer come to the sermons, Inigo.

XAVIER   The Cardinal of Trani and Dean of the Sacred College have declared that we are just wolves in sheep's clothing. Others say that you are on the run from the Inquisition, Inigo.

FAVRE   Some of our one-time supporters have subtly distanced themselves from us.

BOBADILLA   Look, let's just say it straight: Everyone hates us. And our bloody, heroic work has just been trashed by the rich and powerful. And everyone else.

XAVIER   Is it all over?

Pause. They look at one another.

INIGO   I see. So for the first time in my life I must run away in shame and defeat. I see. *(Pause)* Never. The Enemy is fighting us with the greatest opposition he can. But the hotter the forge, the tougher the metal. I will go head on. I will go directly to the Pope and tell him of my brushes with the Inquisition. In Alcala, in Salamanca, Paris and Venice. I will tell him I have been in prison several times on suspicion of heresy.

XAVIER   But why, Inigo?

INIGO   Because I don't want any of our enemies to inform the Pope of these matters in greater detail. I don't want anyone to demand a more thorough investigation of the allegations against me.

BOBADILLA   Good. That's good. Canny.

INIGO   That is why I will insist on a thorough investigation of me. Myself.

BOBADILLA   What? Are you crazy, man?

FAVRE   Is this wise, Inigo? With the way things are now?

BOBADILLA   Wise? It's lunacy. We won't let you do it.

INIGO   I have never run away in my life. I want a final judgement as to my orthodoxy. I will not tolerate one further slur on our little company.

XAVIER   But if you should lose, dear Inigo?

INIGO   We will win. We will. We must confront this head on. We must face and defeat the Enemy. He is now circling our fortress' citadel to find any cracks in our walls. We are under siege. Outnumbered. But let us show our Lord what we are made of. Yes. It looks impossible I agree. But we mustn't be scared. No fear. We must act. Because to God, and us his little warriors, nothing is impossible.

They all look at one another.

BOBADILLA   Inigo. I know you never wanted to but perhaps now is the time we should think about enlisting powerful and influential allies.

INIGO   No.

XAVIER   This is a very important issue Bobadilla and we need to—

BOBADILLA   We need to come out with all guns blazing. This is good versus evil. Wake up!

INIGO   I have always resisted enlisting such power.

FAVRE   Perhaps we should use the decision making techniques from the *Exercises* and make a group discernment. Then put it to a majority vote as usual.

XAVIER   Perhaps we could just use the pro contra exercise, Inigo.

FAVRE   Yes. And wear the imaginary masks of strangers to put the arguments and hear with God's ears?

XAVIER   Or the exercise where we reflect on what decision we wished we had made when on our death bed.

FAVRE   Yes.

Pause.

XAVIER   Inigo, Brothers. We seek perspective in this matter. Like our brother artist friends seeking new dimensions, new perspectives. Our reflections are full of the newness of the age. They are new. A ship to Jerusalem has mysteriously been denied us. So let us sail forward bravely, to the interior Holy Land. To the New World of the soul, using the *Exercises* as our map.

INIGO   I have criticised others for courting power. I have seen others set out on this voyage and, without even knowing it is happening, they have been befogged and dashed on the rocks of temporal gain.

XAVIER   O yes. Once we have set sail on such a route there will be no turning back. It will take an heroic strength of mind and spirit to remain radical and untainted.

BOBADILLA   What are we? Children? Idiots? Are we all going to sell our souls to the Devil just because we are clever enough to get some powerful help for our good cause? It's ridiculous. What's to discern? *(They all look at him)* Sorry.

INIGO   This is a game of joust with the Evil One. I can smell the stench of his tilt-yard. A deadly game. And one which I doubt we can win.

They all stare at him and one another.

BOBADILLA   But Inigo, can you now see our good work sacrificed on the altar of your principles? Is this just a subtle form of pride? A re-visiting of your youth when you were so puffed up with empty vainglory? Is this just the destructive spirit masquerading as goodness?

XAVIER   How dare you talk to Brother Inigo like that?

INIGO   No, Xavier. There is much wisdom in Bobadilla's words.

BOBADILLA   There is?

INIGO   Very well. We will discern using the *Exercises. (Beat)* So. Do we court power or not?

They close eyes. Breathe.

Lights fade. Music

A COURT ROOM. ROME. 1538.

INIGO in the dock. ISABEL ROSER, FAVRE and XAVIER are present. As is GIAN CARAFA, in the gallery.

CLERK   Please be upstanding for Benedetto Conversini, Bishop of Bertinoro and Governor of Rome.

CONVERSINI enters, followed by a NOTARY.

CONVERSINI You swear on the Bible that all you will utter is true before God?

INIGO   I so swear.

CONVERSINI How many times have you been on trial, Loyola?

INIGO   This is the eighth time, your Reverence.

CONVERSINI I fear this may be your last, Loyola.

INIGO   It is my hope. Not my fear, your Reverence.

CONVERSINI So. First, your '*Spiritual Exercises*'.

INIGO   Have you made them, your Reverence?

CONVERSINI I have studied them closely.

INIGO   But they are to be made not just read. Otherwise it would be like a man looking at a map and never going to the place to which it refers.

CONVERSINI So. Your '*Spiritual Exercises*'. You seek to combine contemplation and action?

INIGO   Yes, your Reverence.

CONVERSINI You have confidence in the emotional, affective experience of God's love?

INIGO   Yes, your Reverence.

CONVERSINI Would you concede that this kind of discernment undermines respect for reason, learning and authority, Loyola?

INIGO   No. We value reason, learning and authority too. As our collective qualifications in theology and philosophy would suggest. And our respect for authority is attested to by the fact that I have insisted on this trial.

CONVERSINI   You seek divine guidance in all decisions, even the most mundane details?

INIGO   Yes, your Reverence. We try to find God in all things. All people.

CONVERSINI   The '*Exercises*' seem to offer a training in mental prayer and aim to interiorise the Christian life. Yes?

INIGO   Yes, your Reverence. But always with a practical application.

CONVERSINI   So on all these fundamental points you concur with the Alumbrados? The 'Illuminated'. The heretics. Yes?

INIGO   No. Unlike them, we do not favour mental prayer above vocal prayer. Unlike them, we do not criticise external forms of worship *per se*, but rather the unquestioning, unexamined attitudes that can lie behind them. And we give a central place to the Passion which the Alumbrados and others deplore.

CONVERSINI   I have sworn testimonies and witness statements concerning the sudden transformations of those who take the *Exercises*. Novices giving impassioned homilies, people consumed with wild enthusiasm. You are aware of this response?

INIGO   Yes, your Reverence. In a few cases.

CONVERSINI   But could this not also be seen as signs of Illuminism and the work of the Devil who gives spiritual gifts easily in order to lead many astray?

INIGO   No. The *Exercises* stress the importance of common sense in this matter.

CONVERSINI   I also have reports that many tradespeople such as a cobbler and a cook who, due to this mania, have plied their trade less effectively. How would you answer that?

INIGO   I would rather eat a pie made by someone who had made the *Exercises*.

CONVERSINI   Are you being facetious, Loyola?

INIGO   No, it may well taste better.

CONVERSINI   Why?

INIGO   Because it would have been made by someone who was there fully in the present. With all attention. One mindful act is worth a thousand done half-heartedly.

CONVERSINI   So you can find God in a pie, Loyola?

INIGO   Oh yes.

CONVERSINI   Some may argue that the erring ways of tradespeople are of no great import. However, several gentlemen of influence have been reported as losing their way as a result of these *Exercises*. A dear friend of mine, a Caballero to the King, made them and testifies that instead of being a better Christian he became a poorer knight. In my experience the *Exercises* turn soldiers into women. Isn't this true, Loyola?

INIGO   If this is true I welcome it.

CONVERSINI   You welcome it, Loyola?

INIGO   We have much to learn from women, your Reverence.

CONVERSINI   Do we really, Loyola?

INIGO   Very much so, your Reverence.

CONVERSINI   This is in itself subversive.

INIGO   Jesus welcomed all women, if this is subversive, then Christ Himself is subversive.

CONVERSINI *(to NOTARY)* "Christ. Is. Subversive." You have that in the record?

CONVERSINI I see. I have testimonies to the effect that, like the Alumbrados, many people of all stations and degree who have made these *Exercises* are being led in their enthusiasm to abandon their responsibility to work, home and family.

INIGO The vast majority respond well, your Reverence.

CONVERSINI So. For the public record. You hereby defend all that is in your *Exercises* as being of God, Loyola?

INIGO Yes. I believe no person of goodwill and free of disordered attachments will be able to make them and remain unchanged.

CONVERSINI Your fabled modesty, eh Loyola? *(Beat)* Many say you are a Lutheran. *(INIGO smiles)* You find that amusing? The death penalty is a thing of levity?

INIGO Death holds no fear for me, good Conversini.

CONVERSINI Are you quite sure, Loyola?

INIGO *(looks deeply into his eyes, smiling)* I anticipate it with joy.

CONVERSINI *(unsettled)* Good for you. So. Your Lutheranism?

INIGO My alleged Lutheranism.

CONVERSINI Your alleged Lutheranism.

INIGO I pray for Brother Luther.

CONVERSINI Brother Luther?

INIGO Yes. We both want reform. The Church is my family. A damaged family perhaps. Reform is essential. Too much laxity. Too much corruption. But my reform will take place within. Within the individual and within the Church. But never without the Church. To whom I am a most loyal son. And it has never been proved otherwise.

CONVERSINI   As yet, Loyola. As yet. So the Church is corrupt is it? How are you and your group so different?

INIGO   In our Spirituality. Founded on the *Exercises*. In being contemplatives in action. In that none of us will be bishops or cardinals. In embracing the new spirit of the age. Meditation and reflection but fully engaged with the physical world. Immersed in science, philosophy, the arts. No fixed penalties. No rule of enclosure. No sung office. The time saved will be used in our mission. No written constitutions, just the inner law of divine love. Travelling light. We will all live as equals. Unencumbered by attachments to worldly possessions, comfort and security. Ready to go anywhere in the world at a moment's notice to serve others. Breaking free from the cloister. God's men of action.

Beat.

CONVERSINI *(dry)* Goodness me. So. You reject most of the traditions of all preceding and current orders.

INIGO   We have discerned that our way of proceeding must be different. New.

A PAGE enters – hands CONVERSINI a note.

CONVERSINI   This is most irregular. Very well. Admit him.

FIGUEROA (whom we saw as Inquisitor of INIGO earlier) enters.

CONVERSINI   Regent Doctor Figueroa. You are most welcome.

FIGUEROA   Thank you. This is an honour, Governor Conversini.

CONVERSINI   I am an unworthy servant of God, Regent Doctor. What brings you to us today?

FIGUEROA   I interrogated this man about thirteen years ago. For the Inquisition. Several times. I see you're still causing trouble, eh Loyola?

CONVERSINI   You came to Rome especially to attend this judicial hearing?

FIGUEROA   No. That's the extraordinary thing. I'm here in Rome on an unrelated papal matter and heard of this hearing.

CONVERSINI   Have you anything to say of Loyola?

FIGUEROA   Oh yes. He's quite the most stubborn person I've ever met.

CONVERSINI   Yes. Indeed.

FIGUEROA   And one of the rudest.

CONVERSINI   I concur, Doctor Figueroa.

FIGUEROA   Obsessive.

CONVERSINI   Yes.

FIGUEROA   Argumentative. Just like his brethren.

CONVERSINI   Oh yes.

FIGUEROA   Elusive.

CONVERSINI   Thank you. Good. Well, that will all be noted against Loyola.

FIGUEROA   Against? He is one of the best men it has ever been my privilege to meet.

CONVERSINI   Privilege?

FIGUEROA   His '*Spiritual Exercises*'. I read it first as evidence against him. Now I have made them myself. It is a revolutionary little masterpiece of the soul.

CONVERSINI   But –

FIGUEROA   This man has been persecuted enough. It is almost of a miraculous nature that I just happened to be in Rome at the time of this hearing.

CONVERSINI   Merely a coincidence, surely.

FIGUEROA   If it was just me. Possibly. But I have testimonies here from two other former Inquisitors who have questioned him. Both of whom are in Rome at the moment on unrelated business. They persecuted him too. Now they are among his most fervent supporters. Here are their testimonies. *(Hands them over to Conversini, who looks at them.)* I refer to Ory, from the Paris investigation and the Vicar-General de Dotti from the Inquisition in Venice. You will see that, not only do they find him free of heresy, but, like me they attest to the faithfulness and holiness of this man.

CONVERSINI   What is the point you are making to this hearing, Doctor Figueroa?

FIGUEROA   That three previous inquisitors have now become firm supporters of Loyola. As well as these testimonies, I have a list of some of the people from whom these little poor Companions have managed to enlist support.

CONVERSINI *(pause)* Proceed.

FIGUEROA *(reads from a list)* The Duke Ercolle II d'Este, enthusiastically recommends the Companions to his brother Cardinal Ippolito d'Este as well as to other members of the Papal Curia in Rome. The Council of Ancients in Parma have argued in favour of the Companions before the Countess of Santa Fiora, Constanza Sforza. One of the Companions, Broët, successfully gained the support of the Archbishop of Siena and Cardinal Bonifacio Ferreri, the acting Papal Legate in Bologna. The Duke of Ferrara who, after being petitioned by another of the Company of Jesus, Father Le Jay, has stated that God himself is being dishonoured by what is being done to Loyola. King John II of Portugal has petitioned the Pope to support the company and has invited Francis I of France and Emperor Charles V to support his request by making similar petitions of their own. Shall I go on?

CONVERSINI   We have been busy, haven't we, Loyola?

INIGO   My enemies have been busy besmirching our work and slandering our name without reply for many years. I have belatedly learned the importance of this support. *(Looks at the Companions)* But I have learned well, good Bishop Conversini.

Long pause. CONVERSINI stares intently at INIGO, weighing up his options.

CONVERSINI   Testimonies from three such respected witnesses should not be ignored. Hearing concluded. For now.

FIGUEROA   Congratulations, Loyola.

The COMPANIONS and ISABEL are jubilant. INIGO cuts them off.

INIGO *(quiet, calm)* No. This will not do.

FIGUEROA   Loyola!

CONVERSINI   Not do?

INIGO   No. I want a full, formal and final written refutation of any and all accusations. Or I demand to be charged. This must be settled. Now.

CONVERSINI   You have this current Pope on your side. But there will be others, Loyola.

INIGO   I welcome persecution and slander of my name as an opportunity to grow in humility, Bishop Governor. But not my faith. Or my work.

CONVERSINI   Bravo. You shall have your written refutation. Court dismissed.

CONVERSINI exits. INIGO, the COMPANIONS and FIGUEROA celebrate. They congratulate Inigo, leave.

The next short exchange is cut, if the final CARAFA scene is included.

[*CARAFA *(stepping forward)* Congratulations Loyola. I see you have dispensed with your usual form of address to your superiors, Loyola. No more "pal", "friend" or "brother"?

INIGO   I hope I have matured since our first meeting your Eminence.

CARAFA   Or merely the newly found conformity of the erstwhile radical. It comes to us all, Loyola. You'll see. I shall continue to watch your progress with great interest. *(He leaves)*]

ISABEL ROSER is now alone with INIGO. She goes to him.

INIGO   So.

ISABEL   Look at you. Look how far you've come.

INIGO   And you.

ISABEL   Where are you? In your heart?

INIGO   I'm still trying... to find a way... to understand God's denial of Jerusalem.

ISABEL   I know.

INIGO   And you?

ISABEL   Still looking. Still searching.

INIGO   Yes.

ISABEL   You know I want to join your – company Inigo.

INIGO   I do.

ISABEL   Will this be possible?

INIGO   Yes. I will put it to the Companions for group discernment and majority vote.

ISABEL   Thank you Inigo. I thought you may have forgotten all about me.

INIGO   Forget you? If I forget you I can expect to be forgotten by my creator, Isabel.

They join the celebrations.

Lights fade to:

CARDINAL'S RESIDENCE. ROME. 1539.

This entire scene was cut in the original production.

CARAFA   That look of smug victory on Loyola's face at the trial. Well. He may have wriggled away again this time, but we can at least destroy this order of his. And we must, Carlo. For the good of souls.

CARLO   Yes, Uncle. We're liaising with some of the most powerful figures in Rome to strongly oppose, on canonical and theological grounds, their proposed new order.

CARAFA   "The Company of Jesus". The sin of pride. Naming his order after Jesus. Good work, Carlo.

CARLO   We approached Cardinal Contarini to oppose the five chapter outline for his order.

CARAFA   Yes. His order! Back in Paris he said he never would found an order. The man's a liar. An order indeed. *(Beat)* Contarini. Yes?

CARLO   Apparently Contarini has made the *Exercises* with Loyola and is now himself a supporter too, and he was asked by Loyola to present the draft to His Holiness, who said "The finger of God is here."

CARAFA   Loyola. That scheming bastard! You fool. What about your network? Didn't you have intelligence on Cardinal Contarini?

CARLO   Our intelligence is excellent.

CARAFA   So?

CARLO   Apparently Loyola asked him to keep their association secret.

CARAFA   Devious Spaniard!

CARLO   Well, I suppose he knew you would get to him otherwise. Can't really blame him.

CARAFA   Can't blame him?

CARLO   Sorry, Uncle.

CARAFA   Always insinuating yourself in, pushing for a cardinal's hat. You'll be lucky to wear the biretta of a country parson. I gasp at your political ineptitude. Call yourself a Carafa?

CARLO   Sorry, Uncle. There is some good news.

CARAFA   I'm waiting.

CARLO   Several cardinals and bishops are incommoded by this arriviste and his arrogant crew and we work on all fronts to bring him to destruction.

CARAFA   Something concrete. Please.

CARLO   Yes Uncle. How about Cardinal Guiddiccioni, the Bishop of Teramo?

CARAFA   Yes. An esteemed and dignified canonist. We are on friendly terms.

CARLO   More concretely, he is deliciously inflexible and opposed to any more new orders at all. Ever.

CARAFA   Yes.

CARLO   Yes. So our insiders here at the Curia gently nudged His Holiness to make him the arbitrator of the approval of Loyola's order.

CARAFA   Come here, nephew. *(CARLO goes to him. CARAFA kisses him)* I think scarlet is your colour.

CARLO   Thank you, Uncle.

A MESSENGER enters. Whispers to CARLO.

CARAFA   What is it?

CARLO   He's here.

CARAFA   Who? Who's here?

CARLO   Loyola.

CARAFA   Now? But he hasn't been summoned?

CARLO   No. A sneak attack, perhaps? Typical Loyola.

CARAFA   Good. Show him in.

MESSENGER exits.

CARLO   What shall we say?

CARAFA   Silence, Carlo. Leave this to me.

INIGO enters, with BOBADILLA, their ragged clothes finding contrast again with Carafa's resplendent attire and palatial surroundings.

BOBADILLA *(whispered aside to INIGO)* Just keep your temper, dear Inigo.

INIGO   Bobadilla –

BOBADILLA   I know how much he's grieved you but just keep calm. Difficult for us choleric types, I know.

INIGO *(calm)* For many years now I have worked to be master of my passions, Bobadilla. But thank you for your advice.

BOBADILLA   Welcome, hombre. *(He pats INIGO on the shoulder)* Deep breaths.

CARAFA   Typical Spaniards. Always plotting. Stop whispering. Come here.

They approach the throne. Bow.

INIGO   Your Eminence. Cardinal Carafa.

BOBADILLA   Your Eminence.

CARAFA   Ah. I see you have dispensed with your usual form of address to your superiors, Loyola. No more "pal", "friend" or "brother"?

INIGO   I hope I have matured since our first meeting, your Eminence.

CARAFA   Good.

INIGO   I now know how much these titles mean to people.

CARAFA   Ah. There's the little dig.

INIGO   No, your Eminence. I now see how naive I was when we first met. Advising you about your order. I meant well but I can see how it might have offended you and I'm sorry.

CARAFA   No offence, Loyola.

INIGO   I now truly know the importance of fitting in with the custom of a place. Or personality.

CARAFA   Like a spy? A shape shifter?

INIGO   No, your Eminence. To speak the language of the person with whom you wish to communicate.

CARAFA   Or merely the newly found conformity of the erstwhile radical. It comes to us all Loyola. I recognise your little friend.

BOBADILLA   Little? With this gut? *(They all look at him)* Sorry. Nervous.

CARAFA   Have we met?

BOBADILLA   Yes sir, may it please your Eminence. We met you when we visited the Pope to gain permission for our move to the Holy Land, your Eminence. Your Eminence was more than gracious to us all. My mum and dad are still boasting to everyone in our village about it. Nicolas Bobadilla at your service.

CARAFA   Ah yes. *(Beat)* What do you want, Loyola?

INIGO   I want to thank you for the kindness you have shown to our little group of Companions.

CARAFA   Dispense with the pretence, Loyola. I know you've applied for papal approval for a new religious order. Your – 'Company of Jesus'.

INIGO   Yes.

CARAFA   You told me back in Paris that you would never have an order.

INIGO   Things have changed.

CARAFA   So I see.

INIGO   We had been accused of starting an order without apostolic authority. Even though we hadn't. Our decision was actually prompted by you, Your Eminence.

CARAFA   Me?

INIGO   Yes. When you asked Broët and Rodrigues to go to reform the monastery at Siena. Our first papal mission!

CARAFA   Didn't cause a rift I hope?

INIGO   We did discuss going our separate ways, yes.

CARAFA   I am grieved to hear it.

INIGO   But we realised how close we were as a group no matter how far we were separated. We prayed, fasted, deliberated and made the *Exercises*. After month upon month of rigorous group discernment we saw this was God's will for us. Founding an order. Based in Rome. But a new kind of order. Radically different.

CARAFA   Ah yes.

INIGO (*quiet, calm*) When our little Company of Jesus came here to Rome, after a life-threatening journey from Paris to Venice on foot over the Alps and through storms and persecution, the Eternal City suffered heart-breaking pangs of hunger. The dying lay in the streets, the starving children begged in doorways. Within a very short space of time the Companions had housed hundreds of poor in the Frangipani house, fed and tended them with love. We welcomed all. We shared our beds with lepers because nowhere else would have them. These Masters of Theology and philosophy up to their elbows cleaning toilets and vomit. We worked tirelessly to provide an education for children. All the while nourishing our inner life by contemplation and meditation. This is what we have always done. But a – thrill of astonishment shook the city. Merely because we did what is needed of us. This, in a city like Rome, had become remarkable. Cardinals came by night to gaze in wonder at this unusual devotion. To us – it was usual. Yes. The Church needs to be healed and changed. And so does the world.

Beat.

CARAFA   I think you might still find it a challenge, Loyola.

INIGO   I'm sure, your Eminence. How are things with your order, the Theatines?

CARAFA   Well enough, Loyola. *(Beat)* Why are you here?

INIGO   To thank you for your kind offers of posts and positions of power and influence here in Rome.

CARAFA   You are welcome. I admire your brethren, Loyola.

INIGO   But it is with the greatest respect that we must decline all such offers.

CARAFA   Really? Why?

INIGO   They would distract us from the ever-increasing demands on our time.

CARAFA   Ah yes. It must be difficult to be so in demand, Loyola.

INIGO   There are so few of us. We allow ourselves only three or four hours sleep a night to meet the challenges we already have.

BOBADILLA   Yes we're all sleepwalking around like knackered horses. *(INIGO looks at him. As do CARAFA and CARLO.)* Sorry. Inappropriate.

INIGO   And we therefore decline with the utmost gratitude and in profound respect for your person and the dignity of your office, your Eminence.

CARAFA   I see. Very impressive. Now you speak like the minor Spanish nobleman you are. Politesse. Courtly manners, eh, Loyola?

INIGO   I show my respect, your Eminence.

CARAFA   Can't you see how you insult me?

INIGO   No, your Eminence.

CARAFA   You refuse promotions for your followers on grounds of them being distractions. The inference being that my own promotion is a distraction and my own order has suffered as a result of such promotion and that you, in all your lofty, spurious sanctity are above such empty frippery.

INIGO   Your Eminence–

CARAFA   Well your arrogance has been noted, Loyola. And not just by me. You are finished, Loyola. You've made far too many enemies. You will sink without trace and your order will never see the light of day. We know you are a Spanish spy – in league with your Spanish Emperor – working to overthrow honest Italians with your base Spanish treachery–

BOBADILLA   That's enough, Carafa.

INIGO   Bobadilla!

CARAFA   I beg your pardon, Spaniard?

BOBADILLA   You heard! That's enough! Don't you dare talk to brother Inigo like that.

INIGO   That's enough. Bobadilla. Hold your tongue.

CARAFA   I'm warning you, Bobadilla.

BOBADILLA   Oh I've had it with your warnings but I won't have you calling Spaniards base. Even if Inigo's a Basque and God knows they're a mysterious bunch – even to us Spanish. Sorry Inigo. But he's the best person I've ever known. Who do you think you are, you pumped-up, peacock-strutting buffoon?

INIGO   Bobadilla, please! Control yourself.

BOBADILLA   You're right. The inference was correct. You've gone astray with your love of power and wealth and intrigues. You and your second rate little order. You started out reforming. Now you need reforming yourselves. The Theatines. Who are you? You're just frightened of us. And jealous. A real religious order with real workers for God. A radical group of equals. The Company of Jesus. Yes! A constant reminder of everything you're not. We'll be going strong when your lot are long forgotten. Because God's on our side. Look at you. You're a disgrace. You and that pathetic, scheming two-faced nephew of yours. You can both kiss my rough backside!

INIGO   Bobadilla! It's not about who's the greatest. Who's the best. You've got a lot to learn. I apologise for my brother's anger, your Eminence.

CARAFA   On the contrary. I thank you, Bobadilla.

BOBADILLA   Thank you?

CARAFA   You've just made my task of destroying you and your gaggle of boors even easier. Now get out.

BOBADILLA (*as they walk to the door*) Well. I think that went rather well, don't you?

They exit.

CARLO   So coarse. So vulgar. Is this the manner of man with which he surrounds himself?

CARAFA (*prays*) Lord, You see this is a good man. But a deluded man. Please stop him, Lord. If any of my acts of goodness, however small, have meant anything, Lord, in your mercy, grant that he and his order will be merely a footnote to a footnote in history. Amen.

Lights fade.

We hear the Basque lullaby from the opening scene. We see the BLACKSMITH in the forge, swinging his hammer. We see LITTLE BOY INIGO.

Lights cross fade to:

31ST JULY 1556. OLD MAN INIGO IN HIS CHAIR, STARING UP AT THE NIGHT SKY.

Marked text may be cut.

INIGO　　　　　　Ah. Stargazing. Since I was a boy I loved to see God's face in the night sky. The face of God in every tiny detail of nature. God in all things. Within the tiny world of me I feel the giant world of these limitless heavens. O God. Take me to you. For many years I have fought against the bliss of dying and being with you as I have so much more to do for you but I'm tired, Lord. [*My body is pierced with a thousand secret agonies. All those years of youthful penitence and rigorous self-denial have scarred me. Foolish. My well-meaning delusion about suffering. But I look up at the stars. I feel you Lord.*] *(He weeps)* And there they are again. The sweet consolation of joyful tears. And I can hear it. The inner music of God, the loquela, hums in my soul. Ah. So much still to be done. But thank God so much has been done. By You. [*From the day our little handful of Companions became officially recognised we became a thousand in ten years.*] Even though when Carafa became Pope he was – less than generous to us. But we survived. [*To fight the Enemy of our Human Nature and his legions who circle the citadels of our souls to find a weak point and capture the fortress of our hearts. Yes. We are warriors. We have raised our standard.*] To oppose the shallow values of this age and walk a spiritual path is to raise the flag against this world. Now we have found more acceptance and I seem to be a mere constitution maker and pen pusher. You know I never wanted this. This rigid – structure. You know I have worn so many masks, Lord. And now. This last mask. "Ignatius of Loyola". Whoever he is. The Strict Disciplinarian. But beneath, I've always been your little Inigo. The little Basque boy from the blacksmith's foundry. [*Little Loyolako Txikie. With all his same old weaknesses, which hopefully became strengths. So much base metal hammered into a little bit of gold perhaps? I hope so.*] People congratulate me on founding this order, Lord. Ha! You and I know I'm not clever enough for that. The enlightenment by the banks of the Cardoner was all I've ever needed. It is, as dear Father Chanon said, all those years ago in Montserrat, it is all gift. A gift from you – the genius of love. I just accepted it. Lord. Lord.

(He breathes with difficulty) Are you taking me?

Can I come to you?

Really? Now? Oh, I long for you.

May I? Am I finally permitted?

But there is so much left unfinished. So many debts. It's all so messy and disorganised. I haven't completed the constitutions.

Ah. Lovely. Take me, Lord. *(Smiling, opens his arms to the sky)*

So much still to be done...

So much – still to be done... *(He dies)*

The LITTLE BOY INIGO dances round OLD MAN INIGO. Then puts his hand on his shoulder and stares up at the sky. We see the BLACKSMITH'S FORGE in the darkness glowing like a galaxy in space. We see and hear the hammer blows. The Basque lullaby is heard again – "Loyolako Txikie Loyolako Txikie", and the light of the stars fades.

THE END.

Aurora Metro Books

some of our other play collections

THREE PLAYS by Jonathan Moore
978-0-9536757-2-2 (print)   £10.95
978-1-910798-77-5 (ebook)   £7.99
978-1-910798-54-6 (Treatment, single play)   £3.99
978-1-910798-55-3 (This Other Eden, single play)   £3.99
978-1-910798-56-0 (Fall from Light, single play)   £3.99

NEW SOUTH AFRICAN PLAYS ed. Charles J. Fourie
978-0-954233-01-3 (print)   £11.99
978-1-910798-79-9 (ebook)   £7.99

BLACK AND ASIAN PLAYS Anthology introduced by Afia Nkrumah
978-0-953675-74-6 (print)   £12.99
978-1-910798-80-5 (ebook)   £7.99

BALKAN PLOTS: New Plays from Central and Eastern Europe
ed. Cheryl Robson
978-0-953675-73-9 (print)   £9.95
978-1-906582-61-6 (ebook)   £7.99

PLAYS FOR TODAY BY WOMEN
eds. Cheryl Robson and Rebecca Gillieron
978-1-906582-11-1 (print)   £15.99
978-1-906582-96-8 (ebook)   £7.99

SIX PLAYS BY BLACK AND ASIAN WOMEN WRITERS
ed. Kadija George
978-0-9515877-2-0 (print)   £12.99

PLAYS FOR YOUTH THEATRES AND LARGE CASTS by Neil Duffield
978-1-906582-06-7 (print)   £12.99
978-1-910798-00-3 (ebook)   £7.99

FOUR SHORT PLAYS FOR YOUNG PEOPLE by Rachel Barnett
978-1-906582-95-1 (print)   £12.99
978-1-906582-79-1 (ebook)   £7.99

www.aurorametro.com